Scotland and the Cold War

Scotland and the Cold War

Brian P Jamison, Editor

Cualann Press

ISBN 0 9544416 1 3

First Edition Autumn 2003

British Library Cataloguing in Publication Data. A catalogue record of this book is available at the British Library.

Printed by Bell & Bain, Glasgow

Published by
Cualann Press Limited, 6 Corpach Drive, Dunfermline, KY12 7XG, Scotland
Tel/Fax 01383 733724
Email: cualann@btinternet.com
Website: www.cualann-scottish-books.co.uk

Contents

Illustrations

CONTRIBUTORS

Major (Retired) Alastair Campbell is a former member of the Argyll and Sutherland Highland Regiment and is involved with the Regimental Museum at Stirling Castle.

Brian P. Jamison is a final year Ph.D. candidate at the University of Glasgow, Scottish History area, completing research pertaining to Scotland's historical experience with the Trident II D5 programme.

Julius Komorowski is a student of Criminal and Administrative Law at the University of Glasgow.

Alastair McIntosh is a Fellow with the Centre for Human Ecology and author of numerous publications including 'Soil and Soul'.

The Rev. Alastair Ramage has been the Curator at the Heatherbank Museum of Social Work since 1993 and was ordained a Minister of the Church of Scotland in 1996.

Professor Willie Thompson is a retired Glasgow Caledonian University professor and is currently Visiting Professor at Northumbria University.

ACKNOWLEDGEMENTS

Scotland and the Cold War evolved from a conference 'Scotland's Cold War: An Introduction', held at Glasgow Caledonian University in late January 2003. The papers published in these pages were presented at the conference. Very special thanks are due to their authors and to others who made the conference a great success: John Powles, Manager of the Centre for Political Song, Carol McCallum, Glasgow Caledonian University Archivist, and Yvonne Brown. I am also indebted to Stewart Kemp of the Nuclear Free Local Authorities and Gordon McCulloch for their contributions to the conference and to John Ainslie, Paul Dunne, Christopher Harvie, and Malcolm Spaven for their input and the use of various materials. I am also very grateful to those who gave permission to quote from copyright material. In the event of inadvertent failure to acquire such permission, I offer my sincere apologies. Finally, I would like to thank Meta C. Jamison and Linda D. Newman for their continuous support.

Brian P. Jamison

Cold War Military Installations

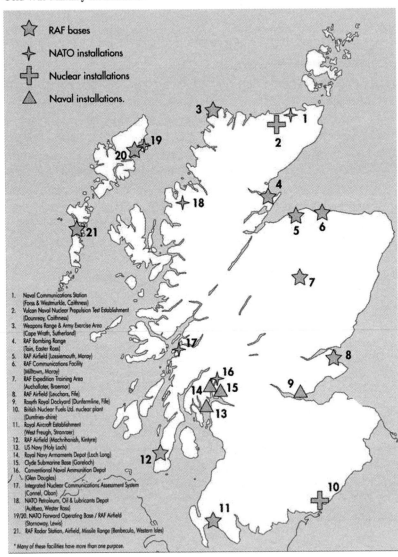

RAF bases

NATO installations

Nuclear installations

Naval installations.

1. Naval Communications Station
   (Forss & Westmurkle, Caithness)
2. Vulcan Naval Nuclear Propulsion Test Establishment
   (Dounreay, Caithness)
3. Weapons Range & Army Exercise Area
   (Cape Wrath, Sutherland)
4. RAF Bombing Range
   (Tain, Easter Ross)
5. RAF Airfield (Lossiemouth, Moray)
6. RAF Communications Facility
   (Milltown, Moray)
7. RAF Expedition Training Area
   (Auchallater, Braemar)
8. RAF Airfield (Leuchars, Fife)
9. Rosyth Royal Dockyard (Dunfermline, Fife)
10. British Nuclear Fuels Ltd. nuclear plant
    (Dumfries-shire)
11. Royal Aircraft Establishment
    (West Freugh, Stranraer)
12. RAF Airfield (Machrihanish, Kintyre)
13. US Navy (Holy Loch)
14. Royal Navy Armaments Depot (Loch Long)
15. Clyde Submarine Base (Gareloch)
16. Conventional Naval Ammunition Depot
    (Glen Douglas)
17. Integrated Nuclear Communications Assessment System
    (Connel, Oban)
18. NATO Petroleum, Oil & Lubricants Depot
    (Aultbea, Wester Ross)
19/20. NATO Forward Operating Base / RAF Airfield
    (Stornoway, Lewis)
21. RAF Radar Station, Airfield, Missile Range (Benbecula, Western Isles)

* Many of these facilities have more than one purpose.

INTRODUCTION

What Was Scotland's Cold War Experience?

Brian P. Jamison

Scotland is usually seen as being a peripheral country, stuck out on the north-west fringes of Europe. To the military planners things look rather different. Scotland sits in a commanding position overlooking the vast expanses of the north-east Atlantic. It lies on the shortest routes by air, sea and telecommunications from the USA to Europe, and it has large expanses of sparsely populated terrain suitable for military training.[1]

These words were written at a time when an American President was intent on leaving 'Marxism-Leninism on the ash-heap of history'. It was perhaps inevitable that for roughly five decades Scotland's Cold War contributions to both UK and North Atlantic Treaty Organisation (NATO) military planning touched every aspect of Scottish life.[2] While Scottish participation in a permanent standing army dates back to the creation in 1661, under Charles II, of 'His Majesty's Guards and Garrisons', some 300 years later its principal

---

Note: The work of Malcolm Spaven and Christopher Harvie inspired the Editor to pursue a better understanding of Scotland's Cold War experience. Both influences have been incalculable.

[1] M. Spaven, *Fortress Scotland: A Guide to the Military Presence*, (London: Pluto Press, 1983), p. 1.

[2] Speech by Ronald Reagan to the British Parliament, 8 June 1982.

role in both a NATO and British military context was to confront any form of Soviet aggression that might have arisen from the north-east Atlantic.[3] From the NATO communications station in Kinross to the Royal Navy's Clyde Submarine Base on the Gare Loch, the 200 plus installations in a country smaller than the US state of Ohio served as testimony to its post-1945 defence of the realm and free world. Scotland offered its airspace, countryside, populace and waterways to assist in this multinational effort; and amidst the physical presence of highly active radar stations, training camps and airfields there were thousands of civilian personnel who maintained these facilities along with plentiful numbers of Scottish recruits for the UK's military services.

The permeating influences of the Cold War for those Scots devoid of military linkage were no less considerable, and everyday living in many Scottish communities was impacted by the groundwork and operation of military installations. For some this provided a sense of security, while others were left with a feeling of vulnerability. As some experienced economic prosperity, others reaped few benefits. Not many of Scotland's communities in proximity to military installations were able to escape the environmental transformation or psychological pressures that accompanied these establishments. Inevitably, during this period civil society often displayed substantial ambivalence towards the construction, existence and function of numerous military facilities.[4]

Though susceptible to academic assessment, Cold War is the term most often used to describe the intense state of relations between the US and USSR from 1945 to the late 1980s, with both superpowers employing client states to further their own unique objectives. At the close of the Second World War the US was prepared to disengage from Europe altogether, but when Moscow extended its control to countries outside the Soviet bloc, an assortment of schemes for a new alliance was

---

[3] H. McCorry, *The Thistle at War, An anthology of the Scottish experience of war, in the services and at home*, (Edinburgh: National Museums of Scotland), p. 5.

[4] For a comprehensive look at the military build-up in Scotland: see Spaven, *Fortress Scotland*.

considered.[5] To counter what the West perceived as Soviet aggression, on 4 April 1949, NATO was established with Britain representing one of twelve founding powers at the start of the Alliance. As a region within a unitary state, Scotland would ultimately serve as an important component within this vast military network and its contribution would be substantial if not disproportionate. Not to be outdone, within four years the Soviet Union responded in kind.

After Stalin's death in 1953, the USSR sought to create its own coordinating vehicle, and partially in response to the admission of West Germany to NATO, it announced the launch of the Warsaw Pact on 14 May 1955.[6] It was the prevailing degree of antagonism between these two great alliances that sustained the Cold War, and it is imperative to recognise that the primary underlying cause of this tension was the unwavering belief in both the Soviet Union and the United States that confrontation was unavoidable.[7] Therefore, it was not supposed to have ended as it did. Perhaps Military Historian, David Miller, summarised the period best when he explained that it was a time when soldiers did not cross borders 'to open the campaign' and 'victorious armies' did not capture foreign capital cities 'to mark the end', thus becoming an era relegated to history with no set dates to mark either its commencement or conclusion.[8]

The Cold War is frequently associated with the potential for wholesale destruction, with both the relationship between superpowers and the advent of nuclear weapons influencing the intensity of Scottish concerns. At a time when the UK, US and USSR stockpiled anything from atomic free-fall bombs to Submarine Launched Ballistic Missiles (SLBMs) with nuclear payloads, Scotland, along with the remainder of the international community, was thrust into an arms race that nurtured a

---

[5] B. Heuser, *NATO, Britain, France and the FRG: nuclear strategies and forces for Europe, 1949-2000* (New York: Macmillan Press, 1999).
[6] NATO-Warsaw pact force mobilization, Washington, DC (National Defense University Press), 1988.
[7] C. Hatt, *The End of the Cold War*, (London: Hodder Wayland, 2002).
[8] D. Miller, *The Cold War: A Military History*, (London: Pimlico, 1998), p. xiv.

doctrine of Mutually Assured Destruction (MAD).[9] In its attempts to maintain security and status Britain had pushed its way into the nuclear arena after the Second World War, firstly through the development of its own atomic weapon and then finally establishing an independent deterrent of medium-range V-bombers.[10] At a time when radiation bombs were still relatively new to the world, British proliferation of these weapons incited mass public outrage on both sides of the Anglo-Scottish Border.

Articles questioning the validity of 'the bomb' inspired the 1958 formation of the Campaign for Nuclear Disarmament (CND), which consequently produced the autonomous Scottish campaign, and yet despite considerable opposition, Central Government, through American assistance, adopted the rocket-firing nuclear-powered submarine as a replacement for the airborne deterrent.[11] It was at this point that the west of Scotland now served as home port for not one, but two Polaris sea-based systems. In 1961 the US Navy had already established its own forward operating base for its deterrent at the Holy Loch, and by 1963 the British Resolution class system, to be stationed in the adjacent Gare Loch, would assist with a multilateral NATO force.[12] Scottish reaction to this scenario was categorically apprehensive, with the stationing of American and British systems in Scottish lochs leading to the belief of many that the country had effectively become a prime target for Soviet military planners. It was therefore a combination of nuclear proliferation and global tensions that, many Scots feared, might lead to a devastating nuclear exchange between London, Moscow and Washington with no

---

[9] MAD was the doctrine of a situation in which any use of nuclear weapons by either of two opposing sides would result in the destruction of both the attacker and the defender.

[10] The bombers were the Valiants (first flew 1951), Victors (first flew 1952) and Vulcans (first flew 1952). The V-Bomber force reached its peak in June 1964, with 50 Valiants, 39 Victors and 70 Vulcans in service. R. H. Paterson, *Britain's strategic nuclear deterrent: from before the V-bomber to beyond Trident*, (London: Frank Cass, 1997). For more on Britain's pursuit of the bomb see: L. Arnold, *A very special relationship: British atomic weapon trials in Australia*. (London: HMSO, 1987). Miller, *The Cold War*.

[11] M. Foot, *Dr. Strangelove, I Presume*, (London: Victor Gollancz, 1999), p. 68-72.

[12] See M. Chalmers and W. Walker, *Uncharted Waters: The UK, Nuclear Weapons and the Scottish Question*, (East Lothian: Tuckwell Press, 2001).

apparent victor. However, there are yet other dimensions of Scotland's experience that must be addressed.

The First and Second World War assisted in strengthening the Home Rule movement in Scotland but what of the Cold War? Scotland's Cold War experience has not been disaggregated in British and international overviews of the period, leaving the correlation between the post-1945 push for greater Scottish autonomy and events within the global community entirely free from academic research. After Armistice Day a Scottish battalion, freshly withdrawn from the trenches in Flanders, 'felt they had borne the weight of the pain and the strife' and were unable to make a desperate show of 'joy and relief'. Accompanied by memories of industrial unrest and 'the Red Clyde', many Scots shared their hesitation at that time.[13] However, during the Second World War political Scotland also expressed aversion when:

> Ministry of Information surveys showed a high level of dissatisfaction with the way the war was being run, verging on disloyalty; these were moreover borne out by vociferous criticisms by MPs both left and right and by the success of the SNP towards the end of the war.[14]

Although Home Rule and pro-independence factions had split, John MacCormick formed the Scottish Convention in 1942 with the Scottish National Party (SNP) winning the 1945 by-election in Motherwell. With discontentment well nourished after consecutive world wars, is it reasonable to assume that some unrecognised amalgamation now existed between the desire for self-government and Cold War? In the mid-1940s the foundations for superpower rivalries were falling into place and by 1949 the Scottish Covenant had successfully attracted some 2.5 million signatures in favour of Home Rule; yet the removal of the Stone of Destiny from Westminster Abbey proved to be the final

---

[13] E. W. McFarland, A Coronach in Stone, (Ed.) Catriona M. MacDonald and E. W. McFarland, *Scotland and the Great War*, (East Lothian: Tuckwell Press), p. 9.
[14] C. Harvie, *No Gods and Precious Few Heroes: Twentieth Century Scotland*, (Edinburgh: EUP, 1998), p. 102.

gasp of the Movement.[15] However, while it is still uncertain as to whether the division of Germany, the first Americans confronting Communists in Korea or the 1956 Suez crisis had anything whatsoever to do with the prospects for devolution at this time, there is a distinct possibility that the appearance of nuclear weapons within Scottish lochs re-energised calls for greater autonomy. In the early 1960s the Berlin Wall was erected, the west of Scotland became acquainted with the US Polaris system and the Cuban Missile Crisis highlighted the plausibility of nuclear exchange between superpowers. With Polaris in the Holy Loch and its British equivalent on the verge of completion, it is not unreasonable to suggest that a link may have existed between these developments and the SNP's historic by-election victory in Hamilton. Though the impact of Polaris on Scottish constitutional aspirations remains undetermined, the UK's nuclear deterrent continues to generate other relevant questions.

Even though Polaris had somehow slipped on to the political backburner by the mid-1970s, the issue of deterrence again resurfaced in Scotland during the early 1980s when Trident, its successor, was introduced. Previous to the Thatcher government's acquisition of the system, the first Devolution Bill was introduced in 1976 but failed in 1977 as the Soviets installed new intermediate-range SS-20 missiles in Eastern Europe. Considering this new threat to NATO and the efforts of separatists, John Erickson, Professor of Politics at Edinburgh University, argued that defence and foreign policy were issues often left unmentioned in discussions pertaining to Home Rule or Scottish independence. He also argued that the efforts of separatists were pointless if the 'waging of war and the making of peace' was left to Westminster.[16] If we fully appreciate the substance of Erickson's commentary, then it is clear that Cold War, and those issues commonly associated with the period, were indeed factors in the drive for greater autonomy though the extent of their influence remains illusive. The

---

[15] ibid p. 108.
[16] J. Erickson, Scotland's Defence, (Ed) Robert Underwood, *The Future of Scotland*, (London : Croom Helm, 1977), p.154.

Trident missile system was no exception. In 1978 the Scotland and Wales Act was passed, and a Campaign for a Scottish Assembly was formed, but the referendum on it in 1979 could be favourably summarised as less than decisive. Triggering alarms north of the Border, one of the first acts of the Thatcher government was to repeal the 1978 Scotland Act, the Prime Minister's 'Scottish' policies providing political tinder. With the devolution issue in Scotland temporarily neutralised, is it appropriate to suggest that Mrs Thatcher's rejection of Home Rule had anything to do with the fact that Central Government was at that time in the process of negotiating with the Carter and Reagan administrations in its attempts to acquire Trident? While the suspension of Home Rule undoubtedly had a lot to do with traditional Conservative Party values, could constitutional change in Scotland somehow influence an agreement over the system with the US government? This is most likely not the case. However, it is fair to submit that political tranquillity in Scotland may have been of some concern for Central Government in its pursuit of Trident.

Despite Mrs Thatcher's attempt to silence calls in Scotland for greater autonomy the nuclear issue, amongst a number of other issues, may have assisted in sustaining the push for a devolved parliament. During the 1980s Conservative support north of the border dwindled as the Trident Works Programme neared completion, and a Claim of Right for Scotland was introduced and a Scottish Constitutional Convention formed. However, by 1992 the Vanguard class Trident submarine had arrived at HM *Naval Base Clyde*, the General Election had seen only twelve Conservative MPs in Scotland and a pro-devolution vigil had been held outside the Royal High School in Edinburgh. Finally, the arrival of the first Trident warheads coincided with the return of the Stone of Destiny, and while a Labour government succeeded in delivering Home Rule for Scotland after 1997, the deterrent still threatened to leave its mark on the Scottish elections though a devolved parliament had no authority with matters pertaining to either defence or foreign policy. Nevertheless, it is important to note that there is clearly the possibility of making something of nothing when contemplating the nuclear issue in Scotland, and there is an abundance of material that supports the arguments of both those who champion the UK deterrent and those who oppose it. But more importantly, there is a massive gap in Scotland's historiographical record pertaining to both nuclear weapons and the Cold War. Volumes of questions remain, with both Scottish academics and research students slow in responding to these issues.

A decade after the Second World War the country enjoyed economic stability not seen for nearly half a century, yet throughout a major part of the Cold War era, the attainment of costly military hardware and installations coincided with heavy industrial decay. Allied ship losses along with the destruction of enemy property initially brought some prosperity to the Clyde after the war, but the future was geared toward the consumption and transport of oil with Scottish shipbuilding companies failing to capitalise. In the late 1950s the coal industry was losing potency, steel imports increased and unemployment in Scotland doubled from roughly 60,000 to over 115,000.[17] Meanwhile, the construction of British Nuclear Fuels Ltd (BNFL) nuclear plant in Chapelcross and the steady production of weapons grade plutonium, as well as electricity, served as an indication of Britain's commitment to national defence and NATO. That same year the Royal Artillery rocket range was also introduced at Benbecula and South Uist.[18] As the North British Locomotive Company was shut down due to its inability to supply modern locomotives, in 1961 a NATO Allied Command Europe (ACE) high communications station, a link system comprising forty-nine tropospheric scatter links and forty line-of-sight microwave links, was also established in the Shetlands.[19] Interestingly enough, by this

---

[17] Harvie, *No Gods and Precious Few Heroes*, p.143

[18] The Uist range position, facing out on to the open Atlantic, also makes it a prime candidate to house the second generation of the US 'Son of Star Wars' defence system, which envisages that missile interceptors will eventually be based in Europe to provide America's allies with the umbrella shield against nuclear attack. T. Crichton, 'Airport aims to lure military to Hebrides', *Sunday Herald*, 29 December 2002, p. 4.

[19] System design of the network was tailored to meet the specialised requirements of Allied Command Europe, which needed reliable, secure and instantaneous communications to link its commanders in the European-wide command area. See *Jane's Military Communications 1987*, (Jane's Publishing, New York, 1987).

time drink and tobacco were well on their way to becoming the leading growth industry in Scotland, and by 1967 increasing numbers of emigrants moved abroad: 16,000 to other parts of the UK and 29,000 overseas.[20] Continuing to follow these trends, the Scottish economy failed to improve.

The economy still struggled in the late 1960s despite the production of Oberon class conventional submarines outside Glasgow or the introduction of Resolution class boats to the west of Scotland. With coal and shipbuilding suffering further decline the numbers requiring assistance doubled between the early 1960s to the early 1970s due to unemployment, an ageing population, single mothers and abandoned wives.[21] It becomes apparent that during this period Scotland discovered that, like the rest of Britain, its outmoded industrial plants could not vie with contemporary commercial production from abroad. Scottish shipbuilding industries were the most apparent failure, and the immense Glasgow shipyards that once delivered great ocean liners became insolvent. In due time, several commercial enterprises once controlled by Scots had been merged into either English or multinational conglomerates. But, did the Cold War play a role in Scotland's economic decline?[22]

While Scottish Historian, Christopher Harvie, and others have thoroughly interpreted the numerous ailings of the Scottish economy in the twentieth century, the study of Cold War economies is still a recent development. The refusal to choose between guns and butter during the Cold War subjected western economies to decades of worrisome inflation, inadequate public and private investment, feeble productivity growth, and deficits that might have overwhelmed their economies and

---

[20] G. Credland, G. Murray, *Scotland: A New Look*, (London: Scottish Television Limited, 1969), p. 75.

[21] K. Hartley, *The UK Submarine Industrial Base: An Economics Perspective*, (University of York: Centre for Defence Economics, no date), p. 4. Harvie, *No Gods and Precious Few Heroes*, p. 158.

[22] For a better understanding of twentieth century economy in Scotland see Harvie, *No Gods and Precious Few Heroes,* and P. L. Payne, The Economy, (ed.) T. M. Devine and R. J. Finlay, *Scotland in the Twentieth Century*, (Edinburgh: EUP, 1996).

politics had the Soviet Union not collapsed when it did. According to Professor Paul Dunne of Middlesex University, during the early 1980s the defence industry in the UK became increasingly important to manufacturing as it 'protected from the ravages wrought on the rest of the industry'. However, the defence industrial base may have supported jobs but it diverted resources from other uses, it crowded out investment from the civil sector and the Military Industrial Complex acted in its own interests and not the country's ' … and invents threats'.[23] Dunne further argued that 'the results suggest a negative effect of military spending on economic growth for advanced economies' and that decreasing military spending 'can improve economic performance, particularly when savings are reallocated.'[24]

Though the discovery of North Sea oil during the 1970s led to 'significant improvement' in the relative performance of the Scottish economy, to what extent was Dunne's assumption applicable to the Scottish dimension and what were the repercussions of constructing military installations, such as the NATO forward operating airfield on Stornoway, at that time?[25] In July 1980 the Thatcher government announced the purchase of the US Trident system, and by May 1985 Sir Hector Monro, Conservative MP for Dumfries, insisted that 50,000 jobs could have been lost in Scotland if the system were not successfully implemented.[26] There was further decline of traditional industry and trade unionism during this period. Unemployment in Scotland peaked at 15.6 per cent by this time and economic theory generally had no distinctive role for military spending. Therefore, it is important to assess what percentage of Monro's statement was political manoeuvring and

---

[23] P. Dunne, *Restructuring of the British Defence Industry*, (Middlesex: Middlesex University Business School, December 1999), p. 8

[24] Dunne, *Restructuring of the British Defence Industry*, p. 8. Nils Petter Gleditsch, Addne Cappelen, Olav Bjerkholt, Ron Smith and Paul Dune, 'The Peace Dividend' in the Contributions to Economic Analysis Series, (Series editors: D. W. Jorgenson and J. Laffont), North Holland, 1996.

[25] See M. Gaskin and D. I. MacKay, *Economic impact of North Sea oil on Scotland*, (Scottish Economic Planning Department; University of Aberdeen Department of Political Economy, 1978).

[26] *Trident*, Parliamentary Debates (Hansard), Vol. 78 Col 509, 10 May 1985.

what was attributed to genuine economic concerns. More importantly, it is necessary to apply Dunne's theory to the whole of the country's Cold War experience and to interpret its effects on Scotland's local and national economies. However, the environmental and psychological aspect of Cold War is also in dire need of attention.

AH64D Apache Longbow helicopters depart from RAF Leuchars in Scotland. The Apache went into production in the early 1980s. *(© Ministry of Defence)*

Cold War military establishments were usually located away from larger population centres like Glasgow or Edinburgh and these facilities often provided dramatic environmental and psychological impact on rural communities. The village of Aultbea on the northwest coast witnessed the construction of a NATO Petroleum, Oil and Lubricants (POL) Depot in 1966 which was used to refuel Royal Fleet Auxiliaries and other military tankers and warships. The traditional holiday resort of Lossiemouth on the Moray coast hosted the RAF airfield sometimes referred to as 'Britain's most important front-line station', and the former fishing town of Rosehearty, four miles west of Fraserburgh, also endured the installation of a RAF bombing range. The weight of pressures accompanying these facilities on local residents undoubtedly varied, but it is also important to note that many inhabitants were willing to accept these establishments in return for the economic benefits some of them provided. However, the cultural conflict relating to military bases involved installations where a large, shifting population of mostly single men were imposed upon small towns or rural areas.[27] There is also an issue pertaining to the physical presence of these installations. Perhaps the views of a Blairmore resident who witnessed the construction of Royal Navy Armaments Depot (RNAD) at Coulport on Loch Long, used for the storage of both Polaris and Trident warheads, best described the understanding of the average resident in the most extreme of circumstances. Living in direct visual contact with the facility, the interviewee explained that during construction:

> It presented a large scar on the landscape of Loch Long. Since that time the scarring [along the shore] has healed slightly as a result of vegetation re-establishing itself on the bare rock and concrete. At Ardentinny you cannot escape from the rape of the landscape.[28]

Those of the area were forced regularly to cope with the presence of Coulport and residents were naturally concerned about accidents, 'but you put it in the back of your mind and get on with life'.[29] Nevertheless, there is still further evidence that suggests other outside influences on the residents of communities in proximity to these establishments existed.

Everyday living in smaller Scottish communities from 1945 to the late 1980s was frequently influenced by UK, US and NATO training exercises. Because the most appreciable feature of land use was the number of bases located throughout the countryside, the influence of defence land use at a local level was considerable. Furthermore, airspace

---

[27] For more on military establishments and the various impacts to Scottish communities see Spaven, *Fortress Scotland.*
[28] Interview with a resident of Blairmore across from RNAD Coulport, (06/11/02).
[29] ibid

and waterways were not exempt from such activities. According to author Malcolm Spaven, also a consultant to British Wind Energy Association, there was 'no controlled airspace north of central Scotland and the mountainous terrain was ideal for low level training', with fly-bys being the most audible military presence in rural Scotland.[30] Naval and amphibious exercises throughout the country were also a regular nuisance to fisherman both for the intrusion caused to fishing and collisions with military vessels. According to the Celtic League, in the period between 1979–1989, there were scores of accidents at sea caused by NATO and Warsaw Pact submarines, with a significant number of such incidents occurring within British coastal waters. The League was also concerned that the loss of Welsh Motor Fishing Vessel (MFV), *Inspire*, and the MFV *Mhari L* from Kirkcudbright in Southwest Scotland were directly linked to American and British submarines.[31] However, these boats inspired other environmental and safety concerns. In late November 1970, a fire broke out in the stern of the US Navy submarine tender USS *Canopus* while at the Holy Loch. The tender carried several nuclear-armed missiles and two ballistic missile submarines were moored alongside; it took four hours to bring the fire under control and three men were killed.[32] More recently, an officer being tested for his aptitude to command a nuclear submarine was in charge of HMS *Trafalgar* when it hit a rock off the Isle of Skye. There was no damage to the inner hull or the boat's propulsion system but the outer hull was badly damaged in the collision and docked at Faslane naval base on the Clyde.[33] While the impact of the military presence on Scottish communities has receded considerably since the end of the Cold War, it becomes increasingly apparent that many concerns still

---

[30] Spaven, *Fortress Scotland*, p. 31-36.

[31] The Celtic League is an inter-Celtic organisation that campaigns for the social, political and cultural rights of the Celtic nations The problem ultimately led to new codes of practice being introduced by submarines and UN conventions to address the issue. For more on this see http://www.manxman.co.im/cleague/subs.html.

[32] For more on this see W. M. Arkin and J. Handler, *Neptune Papers No. 3: Naval Accidents 1945-1988*, (London: Greenpeace Institute for Policy Studies), June 1989.

[33] M. Smith, 'Nuclear sub hit rock with trainee in charge', *The Telegraph*, 08/11/2002, p. 8

remain. Nevertheless, there is a distinct possibility that the experiences of these communities will go unnoticed by academia.

Psynchrolift at Faslane: a source of controversy in the west of Scotland. It was designed to lift nuclear-powered submarines for servicing. *(© Brian P Jamison)*

In addressing Scotland's experience of the Cold War, the current volume cannot evade the concerns inspired by the potential for nuclear exchange. A decade after the end of superpower rivalries, we reach a point where the Cold War is stored somewhere within living-memory. However, while the Cold War is now commonly considered to be a bygone era, British instruments of this quiet war, nuclear weaponry that is, still reside comfortably within the west of Scotland. And while it appears that many take comfort from the presence of a national deterrent amidst concerns generated by radical Islam, there are those who believe the era has been somehow reprocessed and sustained. Against this background, the contributions in the present multi-disciplined collection focus both on scholarship and first-hand personal accounts across a variety of topics ranging from the commitments of the Argyll and Sutherland Highlanders in West Germany to the influences and accomplishments of Scottish Communists during the Cold War era. However, the picture they present is not of an experience which was dramatically different elsewhere: fear of nuclear annihilation; the concerns religious communities and the disarmament movement had with the possibilities for nuclear exchange and the responsibilities of military personnel were characteristic across a range of client states. Yet the way in which Scotland's Cold War experience was handled in cultural terms and its impact on the country's society were destined to be unique. This was partly the result of the contour of Scottish civil society and intramural politics, but it also reflected Scotland's position within the UK and the controlling factors that shaped her individuality during the Cold War.

The contributors have also addressed the question of how far Scotland was influenced by her experience of Cold War. It was, at the least, a complex period of transformation that nurtured influence over Scottish political thinking, placed her regiments on foreign soil, modified Scottish identity and delivered the alarming concerns with nuclear weaponry to its communities. But there must be more. In these essays, a picture emerges where Scotland's role in the nuclear theatre and an atmosphere of unstable peace must be disengaged from the country's experience. The UK's preparations for conflict with the Soviet Union were often conducive to fervent internal disagreement in Scotland, due in great part to the presence of nuclear weaponry and freedoms granted through the absence of heated conflict. Without actual warfare, that binding force which rallied nations was partially eroded, thus allowing greater contemplation. While the First World War was fought to defend 'the great principles of humanity' which were believed to underpin Scotland's imperial mission, after the heavy losses of the Second World War, the Empire, in noticeable retreat, no longer provided the perceptible bond that once captivated so many Scots.[34] Therefore, rather than being simply considered an era of lingering concern, the Cold War could also be described as a period of self-

---

[34] McFarland, *Scotland and the Great War*, p. 4.

reflection for Scotland.

The first essay considers the changing view of warfare within the churches in Scotland. In his analysis, Alastair Ramage suggests that the Just War theory, 'the belief that war must have the establishment of peace and justice as its aim', was used extensively throughout the Cold War but ultimately failed to incorporate the teachings of Jesus Christ. The concept of God as a warrior god was an eccentric development within the Christian faith, but it must be acknowledged that it is a notion that has been successfully utilised by numerous governments. Even today, major figures such as the German president, the French prime minister and the Belgian foreign minister have joined religious leaders in expressing concern about the current American President's beliefs and the place of religion in US politics. Nevertheless, it was not until the seventeenth century that any section of the Church sought to establish a divergent view of war. Ramage argues that church involvement could have been more apparent in Cold War Scotland, but underlines the fact that there were indeed active denominational and cross-denominational church peace groups at the time. According to Ramage, Scottish Churches did have something to say about the world situation and the presence of nuclear weapons in Scotland as groups like the Society of Friends made their opposition to war quite clear. While mainstream churches in Scotland often adopted the Just War theory, Ramage also argues that they did not avoid the situation completely as they realised the government's intentions 'to avoid public debate'.

In his contribution, Professor Willie Thompson explores the historical experience of Scottish Communists during the Cold War. The Communist Party of Great Britain (CPGB) was content with associating itself with the Soviet position at this time, and believed that the USSR had symbolised both peace and progress. Conversely, the CPGB generally viewed Western powers as hostile, with the Party ultimately supporting the Soviets in exercising their right to self-preservation. Throughout the Cold War they worked with CND, arguing that the threat of nuclear war stemmed from aggressive western military objectives, thus nuclear weapons became their top priority. However, as the economic situation worsened in Scotland during the late 1950s, the labour movement became more bellicose, partly due to significant upheavals in the Communist Party (CP). According to Harvie:

> Still subject to 'Cold War' proscriptions, the Communists had retained many of their wartime recruits and in the early 1950s had about 10,000 members in Scotland, a quarter of the party's UK total ... Then in 1955 and 1956 Kruschev's denunciation of Stalin and the Russian invasion of Hungary forced many intellectuals and activists to leave the party.[35]

Nevertheless, by 1964 the Party recovered numerically and the CP believed it was on the verge of a breakthrough. Throughout the sixties the CP was very influential in the Scottish Trades Union Congress (STUC) and by 1976 it went on to elect a communist General Secretary. However, Thompson acknowledges that it would be 'absurd' to credit their success simply to Cold War issues as there were several factors influencing its accomplishments. Thompson is also careful to note that 'Peace' always led its members' sentiments, and it was this which allowed the Party to re-establish credibility.

The CPGB's understanding of the Soviet Union ran contrary to Britain's position as a founding member of NATO, but the Party's prosperity in Scotland ultimately inspires questions about the country's place both within the British and international context. While Scotland was once an independent kingdom that resisted English rule, by 1707 both were unified under one Parliament at Westminster. By this time, foreign trade had emerged as a cornerstone of English policy with the foundations of maritime power carefully laid to protect trade and open up new routes. With these important assets already in place, the Union proved advantageous and Scotland was quick to prosper. Its economy rapidly expanded after the 1750s, Scottish towns grew 'more secure in

---

[35] Harvie, *No Gods and Precious Few Heroes*, p. 109.

post-Jacobite stability', and they gradually thrived on imperial trade.[36] According to Historian Linda Colley, 'A British imperium ... enabled Scots to feel themselves peers of the English in a way still denied them in an island kingdom'.[37] Scots therefore extended their influence abroad over the next two centuries while Britain consolidated its political development at home. By 1815, the industrial revolution had assisted the British in their victory over Napoleonic France, with peace in Europe allowing the Empire to extend itself over more remote parts of the world. At the time, Scots were more willing to 'venture themselves in primitive conditions' than their English counterparts, and the economic benefits from such endeavours spurred 'aggressive Scottish interest in British imperial expansion'.[38] However, upon Queen Victoria's death, other nations had developed their own industries; and as its rivals grew in strength, the UK's comparative economic advantage lessened.

The First and Second World War assisted in this decline. The destruction from the First World War, the depression of the 1930s, and decades of relatively slow growth eroded the UK's distinguished position in the world while its empire loosened during the interwar period. With further loss of life during the Second World War, and Scots no longer distracted by an empire in its dying stages, Scottish calls for greater autonomy intensified as Britain's role within the international community was transformed. However, after the war, relations between the UK and the US were strengthened, Britain attached itself to NATO and remained a major European air, land and maritime power. Economically, the UK maintained its status as one of the largest economies in the world; it had one of the largest economies in the European Union and London ranked with New York as a leading international financial centre.[39] Britain had successfully reconfigured its

---

[36] L. Colley, Britons: *The forging of a Nation 1700–1837*, (London: Vintage Books, 1996), p. 128-129.
[37] ibid., p. 136.
[38] ibid., p. 136.
[39] See P. Steele, *The age of empire: historical events in the British Isles 1714–1901*, (Great Bardfield: Miles Kelly, 2002). A. Murdoch, *British history 1660–1832: national identity and local culture,* (Basingstoke: Macmillan; New York: St Martin's Press, 1998).

position within the international community during the Cold War, but questions come to mind. In a Cold War era devoid of Empire, what did these adjustments symbolise to Scottish society and what were the implications for national identity? Against this background, Alastair McIntosh offers his perspective.

In historical, philosophical and psychological terms McIntosh suggests in his chapter that the Cold War was nothing new to Scotland. He argues that the Battle of Culloden was Scotland's 'Road to Basra', that being an experience of total military humiliation which brought about the forging of England and Scotland into the United Kingdom. However, McIntosh methodically contemplates the psychological cost of this event. Set in the psychohistorical context, he argues that the Cold War was a world that Scotland was pushed into, both agreeably and adversely, through the 'divide and rule' tactic of British consolidation. As Britain went on to conquer the globe, ultimately prompted by 'manifest-destiny', he asserts that the British successfully pillaged the world through colonisation and globalisation, complemented with modern weaponry and marketing techniques. In his essay McIntosh suggests the need for exploring the effects of intergenerational trauma, and proposes that the healing of nationhood should create an ethnically inclusive Scottish national identity that progressively replaces the model of globalisation. Furthermore, he underlines the importance of extending Scottish reflections to other areas, including humanity's capacity for violence, and what is said for Scotland's Cold War experience could very well apply to other nations.

In sharp contrast to this the following submission involves the first-hand experiences of the Argyll and Sutherland Highlanders. With retired Major Alastair Campbell's chapter the focus shifts to West Germany, and because the regiment is a part of the British Army, what ensues is an account of a Scottish regiment's experience in the wider British context. Life for the Argyll and Sutherland Highlander was not generally lived within the walls of a 'British ghetto'. Considerable efforts were made by the Argyll and Sutherland Highlanders to maintain good relations with the local German populace, and, as Campbell explains, being based in

Germany was a particular challenge. Nevertheless, the regiment was there for a specific purpose. The regiment trained to fight a Soviet enemy with exercises focused on a number of scenarios, including the threat of Nuclear, Biological, and Chemical (NBC) warfare. The regiment also had to master the skills and tactics required to operate armoured vehicles, a skills different from other forms of soldiering. Additionally, British Forces based in Germany were under NATO command and numerous organisational matters needed to be addressed. The topic of nuclear weapons also resurfaces. The German view of nuclear exchange varied from that of its allies as it was the deaths of German civilians which hung in the balance. Campbell makes his point clear when he states that 'The nuclear age, whether we like it or not, is here to stay' and argues that the part played by such weapons in maintaining peace in Europe is unmistakable. The Cold War is described by Campbell as 'a time of menace and danger', with events surrounding the Berlin Blockade and Airlift, the Berlin Wall and the Cuban Missile Crisis demonstrating 'this only too well'.

The final two contributions return to the home front and discuss both the successes and failures of the disarmament movement since the arrival of Polaris to Scotland in the 1960s, and an experimental legal defence strategy is presented for the disarmament movement in its attempts to decommission Trident. Because the UK's Trident deterrent was successfully completed despite the collapse of the former Soviet Union, the Editor asserts that it is natural to discount the achievements of the disarmament movement in Scotland. Though the impact of Trident on civil society was compromised as the Scottish public grew accustomed to the presence of such weapons over the course of thirty years, forty years of protest inspired the creation of multinational disarmament groups and actions in Scotland served as a world-wide model for resistance. However, as Julius Komorowski has stated, 'The history of such weapons is accompanied by a history of resistance with the resulting history of litigation'. In his essay concerning the disarmament movement and its attempts to outlaw nuclear weapons, he acknowledges that his defence proposal faces various difficulties, but what he attempts to do is to introduce the reader to his arguments and to highlight potential legal ambiguities. Furthermore, Komorowski asserts that there is a rational basis for citizens to take legal action in order to prevent the harm that could be brought about by such weapons.

While war memorials for the First and Second World War are a common feature of Scottish communities, it could be argued that the remnants of closed military establishments, and even those still in operation, represent some Cold War obelisk honouring Scotland's contributions at that time. Largely unexplored, the country's experience retains numerous unanswered questions and this present work fails to even scratch the surface. What was Scotland's experience with the American and British Polaris systems? How did the construction and operation of military installations during the Cold War era affect the Scottish environment? What was the actual employment generated by such establishments and was there credible economic impact? Though this is not purely an academic assessment of Scotland's Cold War, it is the intention of this publication to inspire greater interest in this topic, ultimately generating a noticeable surge in research and analysis. Detailed knowledge of such events would only further compliment Scotland's already rich history.

A piper from the Argyll and Sutherland Highlanders playing in Korea in 1950. *(©
Museum of the Argyll and Sutherland Highlanders)*

Chapter 1

THE ROLE OF THE CHURCHES IN THE PEACE MOVEMENT

Alastair Ramage

'The Gospel commands us to seek peace founded on justice and that costly reconciliation is at the heart of the Gospel.' With these words the Iona community opens its Justice and Peace Commitment. They are words which can well serve to introduce the main argument of this work: the argument that in the latter part of the 20th century the mainstream churches are rediscovering the emphasis on peace, justice and reconciliation which lies at the centre of the Christian Gospel. It is therefore necessary to analyse the role of the churches in the peace movement and it is necessary to follow not only a biblical construct but also a historical construct.

It is almost axiomatic that any biblical discussion of peace issues should start with the Beatitudes and then include some words about swordplay in the garden of Gethsemane and table turning in the court of the temple. What I think this misses is an acknowledgement of the Jewish world in which Jesus Christ ministered and His source of reference, which was what Christians today know as the Old Testament. It is helpful to offer two antidotes to the view that the Old Testament is one great morass of fighting and killing in the name of God, with little reference to a peace imperative. The first comes from the person who is probably the first historical figure in the Bible (and is prominent in the Koran as well): Abraham. In a dialogue with God, Abraham is shown as saying, 'Far be it from You to do such a thing – to kill innocent and wicked together and then should not the judge of all the earth do what is just'. I can't recall seeing this on a banner at Faslane or elsewhere but in an abbreviated form it would have a lot to say. The other which does appear on banners at all sorts of places is Isaiah's great prophecy of which I can only quote a little: 'They will beat their swords into ploughshares and their spears into pruning hooks; nation will not lift sword against nation nor ever again be trained for war.' That was the climate in which ideal Jewish thought in the first century was forming.

Add into that the revolutionary preacher that Jesus was; who, in a climate of massive racial antagonism could not only live a life governed by principles of love but also preach a gospel fired by ideas of shalom, true peace, wholeness. And a teacher who could declare, 'Blessed are the peacemakers; they shall be called God's children,' and 'Love your enemies and pray for your persecutors.'

Following the crucifixion of Jesus and the first Pentecost the Christian faith spread with amazing rapidity, reaching Rome itself by about the middle of the first century. And not only did it grow with speed but it grew quite clearly as a pacifist church. For two centuries Roman soldiers who became Christians refused any longer to carry arms. Many were martyred for their stance. In 298 AD a centurion called Marcellus threw off his arms and military equipment during a festival for the Emperor's birthday. In front of the judge who condemned him to death he declared, 'I threw down my arms for it was not seemly that a Christian who renders service to the Lord Jesus Christ, should render it also by inflicting earthly injuries.'

The embracing of Christianity as the official religion of the Roman Empire in 313 AD was to change the stance of the church on warfare totally; and it is a change that continued right through until the latter part of the 20th century. In some ways it could be argued that it still persists in the 21st century. Professor Norman Baynes described conversion to Christianity as an 'erratic block which has diverted the stream of human history'. This is not the place to argue the motivation of Emperor Constantine but the effect was vast on Christian thinking. Round about 350 AD Bishop Athanasius, one of the great theologians of the church, was able to write ' ... it is praiseworthy to kill enemies in war.' Indeed in AD 416 non-Christians were actually forbidden to serve in the army.

But it is to another Bishop and another supreme theologian that we owe the stance of Christian Churches both in Scotland and elsewhere for all the centuries that led up to the 20th and the latter half of that century to boot. Augustine, in the early years of the 5th century, formulated the theory which he had derived from Cicero and which has led to the death of tens of millions in the fifteen centuries following: the doctrine of the Just War.

Tyler describes both the acquiescence of the Church to Constantine's concept of God as a warrior god and its wholesale acceptance of the Just War theory as 'fatal encircling of the cross with the laurel'. It is essential to have a clear picture of the broad outlines of Augustine's ideas for an analysis of the role of the churches in the peace movement. He insisted that war must have the establishment of peace and justice as its aim; only rulers have the authority to start wars; enemies must be regarded as human beings; looting, rape, massacres and destruction of places of worship are forbidden and no clergy may participate; there must be no demand for unconditional surrender. Such are the broad points of the Queensberry Rules of War. One is drawn to speculate how many wars since Augustine's time could be said to respond to these strictures of a Just War.

It may seem an unusual development of the Christian faith, but it was not until the 17th century that any section of the Church sought to establish a different view of war. The first two of the three historic peace churches date from this century, namely the Mennonites from 1632 and the Society of Friends or Quakers from 1667. In the 18th century the Brethren in Christ developed in the USA from the Mennonite tradition. All three of these churches have a peace testimony but undoubtedly the best known is that of the Quakers which has undergone many changes since the seventeenth century. One of the simplest is the statement required to be read aloud once a year at every meeting for worship: 'We are called to live in the virtue of that life and power that takes away the occasion of all wars.' In 1993 the London Yearly Meeting of the Society of Friends underlined such thinking in the words 'The peace testimony is about deeds not creeds; not a form of words but a way of living ... We need to train to wage peace.'

In the 20th century notable Quakers such as Helen Steven took direct action both at Faslane and at other bases in West Central Scotland. In her public defence of her action at Faslane in 1984 Helen said, 'My claim is that I had authority [to enter Faslane base], the authority of my Christian conviction that a gospel of love cannot be defended by the threatened annihilation of millions of innocent people.'

But if the Society of Friends stayed true to its peace witness, the mainstream churches in Scotland were reluctant to release themselves from the straitjacket of Augustine's just war theories. Although the first peace society in the UK, consisting mainly of humanists and Quakers, was founded in 1816, it was the First World War which moved peace-minded Christians towards something resembling organisation. Yet here, interestingly, the resulting society was across the denominations. A major peace conference in Constance in the summer of 1914 only managed one day before being dissolved owing to the approaching World War. But out of this came one of the few Christian peace movements which is truly ecumenical and international. As Henry Hodgin, an English Quaker, and Dr. Siegmund-Schultze, a German Lutheran pastor, said farewell to each other on a Cologne station platform, they parted with the words 'Whatever happens, nothing is changed between us.' We are one in Christ and can never be at war.' In December 1914 Hodgin, true to his words, was part of a gathering in Cambridge consisting of Anglicans, Presbyterians, Congregationalists, Quakers and Methodists who founded the Fellowship of Reconciliation (FOR), later to become the International Fellowship of Reconciliation, with branches as far away as Japan. They collectively produced a five-point basis which still stands today. The third point shows something of the thinking behind the FOR: 'As Christians we are forbidden to wage war and our loyalty to our country and to Jesus Christ calls us instead to a life-service for the enthronement of love in personal, social, commercial national life.' No wonder that in later times the American

Fellowship should count Martin Luther King among its members. Despite such high ideals the FOR has seen its share of fights, all non-violent of course, over its seventy-five years of existence. It has, however, continued to challenge the churches both in Scotland and internationally: no easy task. In 1959 Lord George Macleod, then President of the FOR in Scotland and founder of the Iona community, exasperated at the continual caution of the institutional churches, wrote, 'Politicians and businessmen stop when they see the red light and go forward when they see the green. Only the Church is forever amber.' It should not be thought that there were no significant denominational church peace groups. One at least by its nature was international: Pax Christi, the International Catholic movement for Peace. Echoing the pre-war work of Pax, it began in 1945 in France at the behest of Marthe Dortel Claudot, who began a campaign of prayer for Franco-German reconciliation. It had spread to the UK by 1958 and one of its first chaplains was Bruce Kent, a figure who later was very much a leader of peace protests by the Churches at many places including Faslane. Within Scotland herself there were enough church peace groups to allow the formation of the Scottish Council of Christian Pacifist groups in 1937, which was, however, to merge with FOR Scotland in 1944.

The only other significant cross-denominational peace group to have a strong presence in Scotland until the last few years was the Christian CND. Despite CND itself being formed at the end of the 1950s, a specific Christian section did not formalise until 1980; shortly after this, a Scottish section was formed with one of the redoubtable founding names being Roger Gray, the optician whose Isle of Skye office window was covered in peace literature, apart from one pair of spectacles discreetly displayed in one corner.

Roger Gray's name is one that deserves to be much esteemed in the involvement of the Church of Scotland in the peace movement. A member of the Iona Community from 1963 (he died on Iona itself in 1986 during a meeting), he represents an untiring effort to influence the Kirk towards its present stance. In 1965 he wrote, 'I have long been convinced that if the world Church, with its vast potential, and its peculiar access to the power of the Holy Spirit, had been in the vanguard of the peace movement, already the possibility of nuclear annihilation would be as almost remote as a return to cannibalism.' Later in the same year at the Kirk's General Assembly in May, Roger proposed a counter motion to a deliverance which declared that nuclear and other weapons of mass destruction are wholly evil. Roger made it quite clear that despite his own absolute pacifism he was advocating that the Church of Scotland took a stance against nuclear weapons, and that the Kirk should endorse and adopt nuclear pacifism. It was just seventeen years (a very short period in Church of Scotland thinking!) since the General Assembly passed with a large majority the deliverance advanced by a former Moderator, the Very Rev. George Reid. The opening words of that deliverance were, 'The General Assembly affirm the abhorrence of war and their commitment to the Christian vocation of peacemaking.' It went on to urge that the Church should press for the cessation of the making of nuclear weapons and the start of the process of universal disarmament. Four years later ninety-year-old Roger MacLeod who had been the Moderator in 1958 and the only person to have campaigned longer and harder than Roger Gray in the Kirk's General Assembly, saw his deliverance on nuclear pacifism accepted. The second part of the deliverance reads, 'As of now this General Assembly declare that no Church can accede to the use of nuclear weapons to defend any cause whatever. They call on HM Government to desist in their use and further development.' And that remains the official policy of the Kirk. That is one of the motivations that has impelled many Ministers and many more Kirk members to protest at the gates of Faslane; that is what has inspired some of that number to be arrested and to spend long uncomfortable hours in police cells in Clydebank and Glasgow.

George Macleod's deliverance also encouraged Ministers and Kirk Sessions to establish justice and peace groups in their congregations. A similar encouragement was given to the Roman Catholic Church in Scotland by the Bishop's Conference. Statements such as that by Pope John Paul II in Coventry in 1982 helped to lead the way. He declared, 'Today the scale and horror of modern warfare, whether nuclear or not, makes it totally unacceptable as a means of settling differences between nations.' Three years earlier the Pope declared during a sermon in Drogheda, 'Violence is a crime against humanity, for it destroys the very fabric of society. Do not believe in violence; do not support violence. It is not the Christian way. It is not the way of the Catholic Church.'

The two major churches of Scotland have frequently over the years joined together with other smaller churches in ecumenical approaches to the government and others. In November 1983 all church leaders in Scotland signed an ecumenical letter to the Government. The catalytic effects that they hoped the churches' own stance would have is best illustrated by the part of the letter that reads, 'We are further aware of an increasing tendency for those in government to avoid serious public debate [the letter has already talked about disarmament] and instead to attempt to denigrate those who oppose them.'

Fast forward now to the 21st century. The peace testimony of the Iona Community is a required commitment of all its members. Trident Ploughshares has been formed; the mass movements of the 1960s and the 1970s have been refashioned in a way to suit the present situation and people. An affinity group of Christians within Trident Ploughshares has taken the name of the 7th century Abbot of Iona, Adamnan, as their title. And on a very cold February morning of 2001 hundreds of people, including the author of this work, have gathered at the gates of Faslane in The Big Blockade. Among them is not an inconsiderable group of clergy: Ministers; Priests; Monks; Nuns; all wearing appropriate wear to indicate their respective roles in their churches. We celebrate the Iona Community Office, the set of prayers determined for any gathering of Iona Members. Then we share our experiences with our own group of clergy and support the first group of arrests for the ubiquitous crime of 'Breach of the Peace'. Then we celebrate Communion together; no doctrinal differences here. I am passed the bread and wine by a monk and pass them on to a fellow Minister. Then the clergy group occupies its part of the road and those who are in the arrestable group sit down while the rest of us surround them in a circle of support. Soon the first arrests happen. I watch as the Leader of the Iona Community is arrested; then a Minister whom I know to be well over seventy and so on. Finally, sadly, I have to leave to come to Heatherbank Museum, thereby missing the arrival of the then Moderator of the General Assembly. The following Sunday one of our members going out of Church shakes me by the hand and says, 'I saw you on TV at Faslane. Well done. It's time that the Church took a stand for peace.'

And where does that leave the role of the churches in the peace movement? What of the future? Individual clergy and members of religious orders will continue to protest. But do the Institutional Churches continue to rely on the Just War theory? Does the Church of Scotland really stand by its General Assembly resolution? And what effect will that have on those outwith the churches? Or will the stand made at Faslane two years ago by some of the clergy of the Churches in Scotland come to represent the future? Or will it be left to the conscience of individual Christians to witness for Shalom? Perhaps the answer lies in the influence that Jesus Christ, who could hang on the cross and say Father forgive them, has had on the course of human history.

References

Miles Christi, Iona Community, (Membership lists).

Revised English Bible, Genesis, Isaiah, Matthew.

R. Clark, *Does the Bible teach pacifism?* (Fellowship of Reconciliation).

G. Nuttall, *Christian Pacifism in History*, (Basil Blackwell).

H. Steven, *Roger: an extraordinary peace campaigner*, (Wild Goose Publications).

Questions and answers about Nuclear Disarmament, (Christian CND).

What the Churches say about Nuclear Disarmament, (Christian CND).

P. Matheson, *Profile of love*, (Christian Journals Ltd).

J. Wallis, *Valiant for Peace* (Fellowship of Reconciliation, 1991).

Church of Scotland General Assembly Reports (The Blue Book).

Chapter 2

SCOTTISH COMMUNISTS IN THE COLD WAR[1]

Professor Willie Thompson

Since the disintegration of the Communist Bloc and the end of the Soviet Union a great deal of discussion has taken place on the history, not only of the overthrown communist parties (CP), but also on that the non-ruling CPs of the Western world, most of which have either dissolved or radically altered their character. This has applied no less to the Communist Party of Great Britain (CPGB) – probably more has been published on this organisation since it wound itself up in 1991 than in all the seventy-plus years of its existence beginning in 1920.[41]

A lot of the debate has been concerned with the question of how important the organisation really was on the national map.[42] In electoral terms its impact was only just better than negligible – it had a single MP between 1935 and 1945, two between 1945 and 1950, and after that none at all. It did, however, continue to elect a scattering of local councillors, principally in central Scotland and South Wales, and had a few right up to the end. All commentators acknowledge that it had

---

[40] This paper is an expanded version of a paper given at Glasgow Caledonian University in January 2003 on the theme of 'Scotland and the Cold War'. My thanks are due to the GCU archivist Carole McCallum, Brian Jamison, the conference organiser, Douglas Chalmers, and all who made the event possible.

[41] There have been at least five general histories since 1991, together with several volumes on particular phases in the party's history and many articles. A major project collecting the biographies of individual party members is currently underway at Manchester University.

[42] See Harriet Jones, 'Conference Report: Is CPGB History Important?' *Labour History Review* Vol. 67, No. 3, December 2002, pp. 347–54.

significant influence within the trade union movement, and through that to a small extent on formal Labour Party policy as expressed at the Labour Party Conference,[43] most famously in the nuclear disarmament debate at Scarborough in 1960. A number of much broader left-wing organisations were also influenced either politically or organisationally by their communist members, such as the Left Book Club of the thirties or the Campaign for Nuclear Disarmament after the mid-sixties. Some have also argued for a significant influence on the arts and culture, especially in the thirties and the forties up to the onset of the Cold War.[44] There is also dispute as to the degree to which the CPGB leadership was wholly at the disposal of Moscow and how far it acted autonomously. Historians' consensus is that there is no easy answer to this question; but that the most likely estimate is that up to the point in 1968 when the CPGB condemned the Soviet invasion of Czechoslovakia (albeit in very restrained terms) the party always followed the general Soviet guidelines, but within those constraints exercised a great deal of independent initiative in responding to the wishes of its constituency.[45]

Right from the beginning the Scottish component of the party was of prime significance, and a disproportionately high percentage of its membership and leaders were drawn from Scotland, including two out of four General Secretaries,[46] once that position became the top leadership one after 1929. From the end of the Second World War, Scotland, along with London, was one of the party's two largest 'Districts', containing roughly a quarter of the total membership, which in 1945 stood at over 45,000 and by the time of the major disruption of 1965, had fallen to about 35,000. Moreover, the CP's trade union

---

[43] CP members couldn't attend the annual conference, but could influence the votes of trade union delegations.

[44] Andy Croft, 'Writers, the Communist Party and the Battle of Ideas, 1945–50', *Socialist History*, No. 5, Summer 1994.

[45] Matthew Worley, *Class Against Class: The Communist Party in Britain Between the Wars*, London, I B Tauris, 2002.

[46] Nina Temple, on being elected as what proved to be the last person in this office, dropped the 'General' and styled herself simply 'Secretary'.

strength was concentrated in Scotland, particularly among the miners, the Scottish Area of the National Union of Mineworkers (NUM) being dominated in the postwar years by the party and the charismatic personality of its miners' leader, Abe Moffat. In Scotland too were located a number of the 'Little Moscows',[47] where the CP maintained a considerable degree of support among the local public and elected fairly numerous local councillors. One of these areas, the mining district of West Fife and the small towns which it contained, was the parliamentary constituency of Willie Gallacher, MP, from 1935 to 1950.

It would be possible to approach this theme from two angles – either what the Scottish communists did overall in the years of the Cold War, or what they did *about* the Cold War. The latter aspect will be pursued here. There is also the question of how the Cold War is to be defined chronologically. There is general agreement that its beginning can be placed in the mid-1940s, at least no earlier than the German surrender in May 1945, though its roots may go further back; but when can it be said to have concluded? There is certainly a strong case that it did not end until the collapse of the USSR in 1991, but here it is necessary to be more arbitrary with definitions, since to cover that entire span would require a much lengthier paper. It seems reasonable therefore to designate our object as the period of the 'classic' Cold War, between the proclaimed breakdown of East-West relations in 1947 to the Test Ban Treaty in 1963: itself divided into the two phases – before and following Stalin's death. Additional justification for this designation may be found in historians' reference to the 'Second Cold War' beginning in 1979, and the period of 'detente' intervening between the first and the second.

In exploring the history of the Communist Party in Scotland during this period, a major difficulty confronts us immediately. Except at its central offices in London the CP was not very good at looking after its records, and after their immediate usefulness was past they were

---

[47] Stuart Macintyre, *Little Moscows: Communism and Working Class Militancy in Inter War Britain*, London, 1980.

frequently lost sight of – the further down the organisation the more likely this was to happen. The interest of historians was not in the forefront of the minds of party officials. The records of the Communist Party held in Scotland itself prior to the sixties are therefore very sparse indeed, and before the fifties scarcely exist. Those which have survived, now located in the archive at Glasgow Caledonian University, are almost all from the Scottish Committee centre located in Glasgow; there are very few available stemming from the branches, or the 'Areas'[48] in any period of its history, even after the central records become more numerous from the 1960s. Additional Scottish material, however, can be found among the British CP records stored in the National Museum of Labour History in Manchester, and there exists a variety of taped interviews with Party members including some active from the thirties onwards.[49]

It has to be kept in mind that Scottish communists were part of a British organisation which was itself part of a worldwide movement, and as far as can be determined the question of a particular Scottish identity in relation to the CPGB as a whole was simply not an issue. The party in Scotland acted as part of a broader organisation, and as far as we can judge (except briefly at the very end) in perfect harmony – its political activity was coordinated with the campaigns and strategies decided upon in London. The CP did favour devolution in principle, but this was far from being a priority and was conceived as a means of consolidating the unity of the British labour movement, not dividing it. As a somewhat later statement puts it, 'The contribution that Scotland could make to the main campaigns of the Party in Britain has been our major concern, but we have also given attention to questions of a specifically Scottish nature.'[50] In the early fifties a few mildly dissident members did argue for a greater emphasis on a specific Scottish identity

---

[48] An 'Area' consisted of several branches grouped together for organisational purposes – e.g. Glasgow, Lanarkshire, Dundee, Fife.
[49] The project initiated by Kevin Morgan at the University of Manchester and currently in progress.
[50] Report of the Scottish District Committee to the Scottish Congress 1958.

with the great Glasgow revolutionary John Maclean as their symbol, but these ideas were easily overridden.[51]

The Early Cold War

The CPGB's public rhetoric in the aftermath of the Allied victory and of the Labour government's election in July 1945 was of unity – unity of the labour movement in pursuit of social change through its strength in parliament, industry and the community; and of unity between the Allied powers in pursuit of a harmonious and peaceful world order (in which of course it reflected the Soviet priorities of the time, which still hoped to secure a superpower dominance with the United States). An article by the Party's chief ideologist, Palme Dutt, in the journal which he edited, *Labour Monthly*, in April 1945 mentioned 'reactionary forces' aiming to incite 'hostility to the Soviet Union *or to the United States*' (emphasis added).[52]

It has to be understood that the Scottish District, though it was certainly important in the counsels of the party overall, did not possess any separate ideological structures of its own (let alone independent ones) and did not include any of the party's major ideological or cultural figures. It did not at this time publish any regular periodical of its own, only specific pamphlets and a book, *Scottish Prospect* (1956), written by John Gollan, Pollitt's successor when the latter retired in 1956. What it did possess, however, was a sounding board that its colleagues south of the border could only envy, in the shape of the Scottish Trades Union Congress (STUC), in which, thanks to the much greater concentration of communists in Scottish industry and the importance of the miners, the party could make its voice heard in a manner impossible elsewhere throughout Britain. The STUC was organisationally independent of the TUC though not in rivalry with it (and did not use the block vote) and trade unions in Scotland were represented in both organisations. Moreover, the STUC, unlike the TUC, included not only trade unions,

---

[51] See Harry McShane, *No Mean Fighter*, London, Pluto Press, 1978, pp. 242–51.
[52] R Palme Dutt, 'Notes of the Month', *Labour Monthly*, April 1945, p. 103.

but local trades councils, and some of these, particularly in Glasgow, were under effective communist control. In this phase of the Cold War the CP was never able to establish a dominant position in the STUC, but it could always make its voice heard. As Angela Tuckett rather delicately puts it, 'Trades councils provided between 11% and 12% of the delegates; but far more than that percentage were their spokesmen in debates on international relations and peace ... '[53] Naturally these debates were also under the scrutiny of the Scottish press where the full weight of anti-communist public sentiment could be directed towards influencing the votes of the delegates.

It was in the TUC indeed that the Scottish trade union battles of the early Cold War were fought out (and almost always lost by the CP, though far from overwhelmingly), for, rather strangely in view of the industrial strength concentrated in Scotland, Scottish trade unions do not appear to have been as prominent as might be expected in developments within the TUC and the major British unions.[54]

The proclamation of the Truman Doctrine in March 1947 initiated the unmistakable beginning of the Cold War, with US aid promised to any state resisting communist subversion. It was followed in the summer by the announcement of the European Recovery Program, better known as Marshall Aid, from Secretary of State George Marshall, its principal initiator. It was soon made plain that this aid was dependent upon the recipients, governments and trade union centres, undertaking a vigorous offensive against domestic communists – and indeed US envoys were often frustrated by what they regarded as the lackadaisical performance of the trade union movement in the UK.[55]

---

[53] Angela Tuckett, *The Scottish Trades Union Congress: the First Eighty Years 1897–1977*, Edinburgh, Mainstream Publishing, 1986, p. 337.

[54] The Scottish Transport Workers' Union was autonomous of the Transport and General Workers' Union, the largest British union.

[55] See Nina Fishman, 'The Phoney Cold War in British Trade Unions', *Contemporary British History*, Vol. 15, No. 3, Autumn 2001, pp. 83–104. In France and Italy the existing communist-controlled trade union centres were too strong to be undermined, and breakaway ones were formed instead.

The anti-communist offensive in the TUC was initiated with a general circular in October 1948 warning affiliated unions against communist activists, followed by a pamphlet entitled *The Tactics of Disruption: Communist Tactics Exposed* in February 1949 and climaxing with a highly publicised debate at the TUC congress later that year which approved the anti-communist stance by nearly seven million votes to fewer than one million against. Communist or communist-inclined trade union strength in Scotland seems to have made little difference to the outcome, nor does the communist-controlled Scottish area of the National Union of Mineworkers appear to have mobilised very much opposition to the persecution and isolation by his colleagues of Arthur Horner, the communist president of the South Wales Area, elected in 1946 as the General Secretary of the NUM.[56] Again, it might appear paradoxical, given Scottish traditions of industrial militancy and communist strength, that none of the major industrial conflicts over Cold War issues occurred in Scotland[57] – the principal examples were the London docks in 1949 (resulting in the deployment of troops),[58] and lesser instances in London engineering factories and the Manchester area. These observations would seem to support the argument advanced by Nina Fishman – that the trade union conflict between the communists and the right-wing bosses was in many respects a 'phoney war' – neither side wished to push matters to extremes – the CP leadership restrained its militants who favoured all-out confrontation, and the TUC and the right-wing individual trade union leaders appreciated too much the usefulness of communist activists at the grass roots to hound them unduly.[59]

A similar absence of militant action is apparent also in the non-manual unions. The CP in Scotland had a number of teachers within its ranks, some of them in relatively high-profile positions, like Jimmy Hill,

---

[56] Fishman, Ibid. pp. 88–91
[57] In 1947 there was a major strike by Glasgow dockers, but this was provoked by redundancy issues and was unrelated to the Cold War.
[58] See Philip Deery, 'The Secret Battalion' – Communism in Britain during the Cold War', *Contemporary British History* Vol. 13, No. 4, Winter 1999, pp. 1–28.

who was a prominent figure in the Glasgow Trades Council. Another was dismissed for allegedly expressing communist views to his school students. Although well respected, they remained politically isolated figures among their colleagues[60] and had no impact on their union's overall position.

Public Opinion

Needless to say, the general atmosphere of the Cold War had an effect on the Scottish communists as it had upon all their comrades, and what had been a generally favourable perception in 1945 on account of the Soviet Union's record in the War had been very seriously eroded five years later. Scottish records for membership in this period are not extant, but the British membership was down to 38,853 in 1950 and 35,124 in 1951, which would mean a probable Scottish membership of 8,000 to 9,000. The most surprising thing is that the decline was not steeper. The fact that it held up as well as it did may possibly have had something to do with the reality that while the deepening Cold War made the Soviet Union a source of increasing suspicion and fear (and consequently for most citizens, placed communist politics beyond the pale and the erosion of voting strength, where nothing fails like failure, was faster than that of membership) communists continued to be respected in their workplaces, trade unions and in organisations such as tenants' associations, and by vigorous recruitment policies, they remained capable in some degree of reproducing their numbers. Indeed, between 1947 and the beginning of 1948 the party even succeeded in reversing the postwar membership decline and raised its numbers by approximately 5,000, from about 38,000 to 43,000.[61]

---

[59] Fishman, Ibid. p. 102, n. 33.

[60] Steve Parsons, writing on British CP schoolteachers does not mention Scottish ones or their union, the Educational Institute of Scotland. Steve Parsons, 'British Communist Party School Teachers in the 1940s and 1950s', *Science & Society*, Vol. 61, No. 1, Spring 1997, pp. 46–67.

[61] Report to the Party Executive Committee, 26–7 February 1947, CP/CENT/EC/01/06 in the NMLH archive.

Initially, at least in Scotland, even electoral performance held up better than might have been expected. A striking example was the bye-election in the Glasgow Gorbals constituency in September 1948, where the candidate was Peter Kerrigan, the CPGB industrial organiser and a Glaswegian by origin. This took place in the aftermath of the communist takeover in Czechoslovakia, the Berlin Blockade, the rupture with Yugoslavia and the Italian elections where communist hopes of victory were frustrated. Moreover, Gorbals had a large Catholic electorate. In spite of all that, Kerrigan's meetings attracted huge sympathetic crowds – in all an estimated 9,000, and over 100 recruits were gained. The vote was quite respectable too – 4,233 against the winning Labour candidate's 13,706; the party leadership was eminently satisfied and reckoned that the seat was winnable at the next election.[62] All that did not prevent Willie Gallacher from decisively losing his West Fife seat at the general election a year and a half later and ending communist parliamentary representation forever. Three months later the Korean War broke out, with large scale involvement of British forces, and the CPGB was more isolated and unpopular than ever.

The British communists, needless to say, continued to support the Soviet position in every respect and on all matters. Most directly in relation to the Cold War, it focused upon what it described as 'peace campaigning' and in particular made efforts to mobilise the organised labour movement in this direction, which in Scotland meant trying to connect the trades councils and the STUC into meetings and conferences in opposition to the Anglo-American diplomatic and military agendas. In the UK after October 1951 these were represented by the Conservative Party, for Labour lost office in the election of that month (the CP put up nine candidates and lost every deposit). Already by that point the Labour Party was in internal turmoil, with Aneurin Bevan having resigned at the beginning of the year to lead the left of the party in bitter struggles against a leadership indistinguishable from the Conservatives in its Cold War commitments.

---

[62] EC minute, 30 September 1948, CP/CENT/EC/01/06.

Struggles in the Scottish Trades Union Congress

1947, as well as being the year of the formal 'declaration' of the Cold War and all that followed on, also happened to be the centenary year of the STUC. In honour of this anniversary the Congress was attended by no less a personage than the Prime Minister himself, accompanied by the President of the Board of Trade, (i.e. the industry minister) Stafford Cripps. The event was not an uncontentious one, the main resolution, critical of government foreign policy, being hotly debated in front of the eminent guests and lost by the narrowest of margins. The main resolution moved by Abe Moffat deplored 'our increased dependence on American Imperialism' and demanded a 'a real socialist foreign policy in the interests of peace and progress' which would need the 'fullest possible political and economic relations with the USSR and socialist forces throughout the world.' Moffat was seconded by George Middleton for the Glasgow Trades Council, who identified the existing trend of government policy as leading towards

> ... a close tie-up and alliance with American imperialism which would lead to undue dependence on the capitalist economy of the USA and would eventually have a serious effect on full employment prospects in Britain.[63]

The voting was 166 against the resolution, 158 in favour.

In May 1948 George Middleton was elected General Secretary of the STUC. A former Secretary of Glasgow Trades Council, he had recently been a leading member of the Communist party, indeed the Scottish industrial organiser, but had since made his peace with the labour establishment. However, he did not move over to uncompromising anti-communism but in general tried to hold a balance between left and right in the organisation, though inclining towards the

---

[63] Angela Tuckett, Ibid. p. 311.

right whenever necessary. According to the President announcing his election:

> His application for and acceptance into membership of the Labour Party should dispel any doubts that may have existed in Scottish Trade Union circles as to his politics; and in the circumstances his appointment as General Secretary will, I feel, result in the continuance of the responsibility and dignity of the STUC.[64]

The following year a resolution was moved by Jimmy Hill to the effect that 'our economic resources should not be wasted on rearmament but concentrated on peaceful reconstruction' and defeated by 189 votes to 139. Another sign of the times was the debate on the disaffiliation of Airdrie Trades Council for ignoring a ban on attendance at a conference organised by the Scotland-USSR Friendship Society. Protest against the General Council decision was supported by the trades councils of Glasgow, Greenock and Clydebank, but was upheld by 170 votes to 104.[65] However, a resolution calling on the STUC to convene a conference to consider 'ways and means of starting off a great Peace Crusade' was accepted against opposition – though not acted upon.

In that year the Congress President was William Pearson, the Scottish NUM Secretary and a leading communist. In his Presidential address he took the opportunity to declare that the fight for peace was linked with that for higher wages and improved conditions and spoke of 'the deadly fear of the weapons of mass destruction',[66] this in the context of recommending a General Council resolution on the 'Maintenance of Peace', asserting that:

> If nothing is done to curb them these Imperialists will involve the world in war in order to maintain their system of profit-making and

---

[64] Ibid. p. 316.
[65] Ibid. p. 319.
[66] Ibid. p. 331.

their domination and exploitation of millions of men and women throughout the world.

The resolution – which was passed unanimously – actually called for a ban on the manufacture of nuclear weapons and the destruction of all existing stocks, together with international control of atomic energy and resolved to initiate the 'great peace crusade' – but it remained a dead letter. Unions were advised to boycott the newly-established British Peace Committee, a communist-controlled organisation. Pearson, despite being that year's President, was excluded from the General Council by horse-trading in the elections and when a conference was held in October in formal conformity with the resolution (by this time the Korean War was raging) government policy was affirmed and the Soviet Bloc condemned.

By 1951 the CP was much more on the defensive. The President, John Lang, blamed the Soviet Union for obstructing nuclear discussions at the UN. The seconder of the General Council resolution on peace was vituperative, and hoped that:

> Congress was not going to become the sounding board of the communists, the fellow-travellers and others in Britain who talked about peace, who could help make peace but who all the time submitted to the dictates of the overlords of the Kremlin [and hoped that] the movement was not going to be prostituted by people ... who know equally as well as any member of the General Council that the greatest opposition to the peace of the world was not ideologies – it was imperialistic communism emanating from Russia.[67]

A miners' amendment (communist-inspired of course) was defeated by 215 to 114.

Nor was that all. At this Congress a sustained attack was launched against the communist-dominated trades councils. These included Airdrie, Rutherglen, Kirkcaldy and Dundee, which suffered various

---

[67] Ibid. p. 335.

forms of discrimination and sanction, from central appointment of new officers to disaffiliation. Glasgow, however, was the principal battleground. As soon as the Congress dispersed the General Council majority took steps to prepare the seizure of Glasgow Trades Council's funds, dismissal of its officers and whole-scale reorganisation. The Trades Council, however, continued in its defiant ways, passing resolutions in line with the defeated amendment, provocatively protesting to the Prime Minister about the behaviour of US troops and finally taking legal action to stop itself being dissolved by the STUC. The General Council, frustrated in its plans, was forced to set up an alternative body to which it invited Glasgow trade unions to affiliate instead, and barring the miscreants from its membership.[68] Following Stalin's death in March 1953 the tensions began to ease; the rebels were quietly reintegrated, and STUC and Soviet trade union delegations exchanged visits in 1955 and 1956. In 1961, a Politburo member, Victor Grishin, addressed the Congress.

A pattern emerges. It can be seen from the voting figures that communist-inspired moves in the STUC were at this time almost always defeated, and the attack on communist control in the trades councils was extremely debilitating to their industrial strength. Yet what is interesting is that despite the atmosphere of the times, it can be seen from the voting figures that these defeats were not overwhelming and the Scottish communists managed to sustain a level of support that would have been inconceivable at the TUC proper. [69]

Naturally, the Communist Party in Scotland or throughout the UK did not confine its Cold War activities to debate in the meetings of labour movement organisations – there were also strenuous efforts made to recruit support from the general public in support of their views. A conference in Paris in 1949, backed by the communists, resulted in Britain in the establishment of the British Peace Committee, an organisation soon proscribed by the Labour Party, and which was, in

---

[68] Ibid. p. 338.
[69] The absence of the block vote made the figures more representative than those recorded at the British TUC.

fact, a 'front' for the CP. Its immediate objective was to gather signatures for an international petition to abolish nuclear weapons announced in 1950 by the permanent Committee of the World Peace Congress. Intense efforts were devoted to this, collecting signatures for what was generally known as the 'Stockholm petition' in workplaces and on the street.[70] Rather confusingly, a similar petition from the same source was being promoted from May 1951 calling for a Five Power peace pact. Scottish communists active at the time and who have been interviewed about their party careers tended to recall spontaneously the degree of effort they put into circulating these petitions. In August 1951 a group of Scottish pipers was among the delegates to the World Youth Congress in the Soviet sector of Berlin. The British government surreptitiously tried to stop them from travelling to participate. Their protest at the obstruction included dancing highland reels on the railway station at Innsbruck.[71] It was Glasgow Trades Council's protest at the obstacles which had been placed in their way that led to the STUC's action against it.

1956

The events described represented what was probably the nadir of the Cold War in British affairs, but after 1951 and more particularly following Stalin's death in early 1953 and the Korean armistice later that year, the situation eased, and the CP, at least in Scotland, was less politically isolated than it had been. Major issues of Cold War foreign policy nevertheless continued to agitate the British political scene, and the focus of dispute was the proposal to rearm West Germany as an integral part of the NATO alliance. The Bevanite revolt in the Labour Party (in opposition since electoral defeat in October 1951) came to focus upon this issue. The communists were therefore pursuing the same

[70] Over a million people were said to have signed in Britain between March and September 1950. Noreen Branson, *History of the Communist Party of Great Britain 1941–1951*, London Lawrence & Wishart, 1997, p. 210.

[71]. Branson, Ibid. pp. 228–9.

objectives as, even if not in communion with, a large part of the Labour left – though the latter of course did not welcome the taint of communist support.

However, it was the party's intransigent attachment to the Soviet Union and that state's cold war perspectives which disrupted it calamitously in the middle of the fifties. The Soviet leadership's partial *rapprochement* in 1955 with the breakaway Yugoslav state, formerly denounced as a fascist stooge of US imperialism, must have given party members cause to wonder – but it was the events of 1956 that were to mark an unexampled break. [72]

These, of course, were not wholly attributable to the Cold War, since they were partly a consequence of the terror regime instituted in the thirties under Stalin's leadership and which by the time of his death was becoming counter-productive in terms of economic performance and social cohesion. The despot's embalmed corpse had scarcely been placed beside Lenin's before cautious beginnings were made towards measures of relaxation and restructuring. They reached a climax with Khruschev's famous denunciation of (some of) his crimes at the 20th Congress of the Soviet Communist Party in February 1956. The CPGB was profoundly affected – probably more so than most communist parties in Western Europe – and in Scotland the reactions were felt no less strongly than in any other part of the UK.

According to the Glasgow *Forward*, a Labour Party newspaper:

The debunking of Stalin is having serious repercussions among the Party rank and file. They are fighting with one another – to get out of the Party first. In Glasgow alone between 20 and 30 Communist Party members are known to have quit in the last few weeks ...

There is no reason to disbelieve this claim, yet the reminiscences of some party members of the period do not confirm the picture of total

---

[72] For an overall account of the events of this year as it affected the Communist Party, written by participants, see especially the *Socialist Register* for 1976, and Alison McLeod, *The Death of Uncle Joe*, Merlin, 1998.

disruption it points to. One claimed that the Khruschev revelations 'didn't really figure much ... they didn't really relate to our attempt to publicly present the party ... had no direct implication for our activity.' and another, 'it was never a big thing ... '[73]

Much the fiercest criticism though came from a rising star of the Scottish CP district, a young mining trade unionist no less, based in the party's main Scottish stronghold, West Fife, a member of the Scottish Committee and Secretary of his local NUM branch. He declared in the local newspaper that the attack now being made on Stalin was as unprincipled as the former adulation, 'the most disgusting and disgraceful political somersault in political history', and that the party, which did not control so much as a local council on the lowest of levels, would never be trusted politically by British workers.[74]

At the beginning of November controversy over the internal record of the Soviet and East European regimes was overtaken and intensified by developments arising directly out of the Cold War, when the reform communist government in Hungary that had arisen out of a popular revolution tried to withdraw from the Soviet-controlled military alliance, the Warsaw Pact. Soviet forces invaded Hungary and put down the rising with great slaughter, following this by installing a more compliant regime. Bitterness among the section of British party members who now felt doubly betrayed was exacerbated further when the CPGB leadership announced that it was approving the Soviet action. Resignations turned into a flood, and at least a quarter of the party's membership was lost.

Public hostility became intense as party speakers on outdoor platforms at factory gates or on the streets attempted to justify what the Soviets had done and they were always subjected to much verbal abuse. Sometimes they were physically attacked as well:

---

[73] Carol Thornton and Willie Thompson, 'Scottish Communists, 1957-57', *Science & Society*, Vol. 61, No. 1, Spring 1957, p. 79.
[74] Letters to *The Times for Lochgelly and District*, 28 June 1956, 12 July 1956 and 9 August 1956.

I had to speak [at an outdoor meeting] on the Sunday night the Red Army went into Budapest and when we turned up the street was black, absolutely hundreds of them there ... and of course you had a number of Labour Party people. Left Labour Party people ... who used to frequent all these meetings on a Sunday night ... so that was a very difficult meeting.[75]

At a Scottish NUM conference on 12 November the Soviet invasion was condemned – though only by 61 votes to 56.[76] On the ground in the pits the reaction was much stronger. About fifty miners marched to the Scottish NUM headquarters demanding the resignation of all communists on the executive and in full-time positions, and two pits held a one-day strike for similar demands.[77]

That was not all. Abe Moffat's younger brother Alex, though he had 'been a close friend of the Soviet Union for thirty years,' nevertheless found himself 'so much in conflict with the policy, tactics and leadership' that he found it 'impossible in principle to continue in membership of the Party.'[78] He resigned, though rejoining a few years later. Unprecedentedly, when the Scottish Committee came to approve the Executive Committee stance there were contrary votes, 3 to 26, and on a more ambiguous resolution, the vote was evenly split.[79]

There continued to be, however, a number of dissidents who held on in the hope that the special party congress which had been summoned for the spring of 1957 might result in a reversal of policies and replacement of the Soviet-line leadership, but though it was a very stormy event the leadership had the situation well in hand as far as the votes were concerned, and their wishes prevailed all along the line.[80] Not only were the Executive's decisions respecting Hungary reaffirmed, but

---

[75] George Greig, CP official, in Thornton and Thompson, Ibid. p. 83.
[76] *Glasgow Herald*, 13 November 1956.
[77] Ibid. November 27, 1956.
[78] Ibid. 14 November 1956.
[79] Carol Thornton and Willie Thompson, Ibid. p. 84.
[80] By this time Pollitt had resigned as the General Secretary on grounds of ill health and had been replaced by Gollan.

with minimal alterations it was resolved to retain the party rules of 'democratic centralism' which allowed a self-selecting leadership (elections were effectively formalities) to run the party autocratically.

Another bout of resignations followed. In Scotland they included a full-time party official, Donald Renton.

> Because of the tactics of the leadership at [the 1957] congress Mr. Renton states that he found himself with no alternative to resignation from the party he has served for 28 years. Mr. Renton ... emphasised in an interview that he was still a 'militant socialist supporting the aims of the October Revolution of 1917.' But communist principles can only be achieved by adherence to Marxist principles, he believes, and he sees the basic issue before the British CP as one of loyalty to principles and not to leaders. He described himself as wholly opposed to the suggestion that party decisions taken in the Soviet Union should be regarded as wholly right.[81]

The Scottish leadership, though it tried to win back the resigned members by personal visit and persuasion, did not forgive the individuals in leading positions who had shown themselves infirm in its view, even if they had not resigned. Those who had been persistent in questioning the official line at Scottish Committee meetings and then voted the wrong way, or who had carried their disagreements outside closed meetings, were dropped from the Scottish Committee at the next Scottish congress. These included its leading woman activist, Rhoda Fraser.

> The evidence of our interviewees suggests – though nothing seems to have survived in the written record – that this woman had a stormy relationship with the Party leaders, who felt that she tended to dilute a specifically communist message in her campaigning on women's and peace issues.[82]

---

[81] *Glasgow Herald*, 30 April 1956.
[82] Carol Thornton and Willie Thompson, Ibid. p. 89.

Meantime in West Fife Lawrence Daly had assembled his considerable following, consisting of several hundred, into the Fife Socialist League, which he insisted was a separate political party, and was accepted as a component of the British New Left.[83] Its members at once began to win miners' union elections against communists (later Daly was elected Secretary of the Scottish NUM against a communist opponent) and council seats as well. He also stood as a parliamentary candidate in the 1959 general election and achieved a respectable vote of nearly 5,000, a thousand more than the communist candidate, who at 3,828 was 1,558 down on the 1955 general election total.[84]

The party certainly suffered severely for its unwavering attachment to the Cold War opponent, and in the end it was undoubtedly weakened, though, nevertheless, out of that disaster evolved new sources of strength. In Scotland, in spite of everything, the extent of damage to its influence in the industrial field was limited (the outcome of the ETU ballot-rigging trial in 1961 was actually much more damaging in the long term). In the NUM, although Daly had no difficulty in winning any position he stood for, communist control overall soon reasserted itself and his support was too personalised and narrow to break the party's hold on this union organisation.

CND

Even in its damaged state the CP in Scotland still sustained a very considerable presence, with a membership of around 6,000 (not all of them active), continuing strength in many trade unions, particularly the miners, many dedicated activists and, for its size, an extraordinarily large full-time staff located both in the party headquarters in Glasgow and in the more important 'Areas' of the country – principally the

---

[83] This now largely forgotten organisation is certainly worthy of serious study. It was dissolved by Daly in late 1962. There is a preliminary discussion in Willie Thompson, 'The Scottish New Left', in Ian MacDougall, (ed), *Essays in Scottish Labour History*, Edinburgh, John Donald, 1978. See also Lawrence Daly, 'Fife Socialist League' in No. 4, July/August 1960.

[84] CP 'Report of the 1959 General Election', Scottish Committee Archive, Glasgow Caledonian University.

central belt. When Jack Ashton (Scottish Secretary in the seventies and eighties) became a full-time official, replacing Donald Renton in Edinburgh after the latter's resignation, there were over twenty full-timers in office, not counting the *Daily Worker* reporter and the circulation organiser, as well as clerical employees.[85] It had the resources and basis for recovery and development once the political climate became more favourable.

A Scottish CND march from the 1960s *(© Scottish Campaign for Nuclear Disarmament)*

Such a time was not long in arriving, and if the Cold War had damaged the CPGB almost fatally, the Cold War, paradoxically, also enabled it to recover. Massive nuclear armouries and strategies of Mutually Assured Destruction was the logic. A British atomic bomb had been tested in 1952, and in 1957 its enormously more powerful successor, the nuclear or hydrogen bomb, was coupled with the doctrine of 'massive retaliation' enunciated by the defence minister, Duncan Sandys. Following earlier discussions the Campaign for Nuclear Disarmament was launched in February 1958, fronted by major

---

[85] Undated letter from Jack Ashton to John Kay. Ibid.

personalities (none of them Scottish) and leading Labour Party left-wingers (none of these Scottish either), and speedily attracted support on a scale which astonished its sponsors.

Although the bulk of CND's supporters were not from the traditional ranks of the Labour Party – it is generally agreed that it was an overwhelmingly middle-class movement – and its principal activity was mounting demonstrations, especially the annual Aldermaston march at Easter, capture of the Labour Party conference became its strategic objective since conversion of that Party to its aims was recognised as the obvious route to achieving them. The key to winning the Labour Party conference was held by the trade unions, which wielded the block vote, and since the leader of the biggest union, the Transport and General Workers, Frank Cousins, had been won over, it appeared feasible. However, the forces were finely balanced (for official Labour policy was very much in line with Conservative), and, as it happened, the Communist Party was in the position of being able to determine the outcome. This it could do through its influence in the miners' union, not least in its Scottish Area.

The Communist Party leadership though did not approve of CND, not so much on account of its middle-class character, for after all it was happy enough with middle-class support when that coincided with its own purposes, but because it distrusted the Campaign's aims. In short, it regarded them as a diversion. Abolishing British nuclear weapons did not strike the communists as an objective upon which it was worth spending enormous time and resources; instead it wanted the anti-nuclear protest to be directed towards bringing about big-power negotiations leading to their mutual abolition and the institution of a global regime of peaceful co-existence: the declared Soviet aim. At the STUC Congress in 1959 a unanimous resolution was passed in these terms.[86] Great hopes were pinned upon the Khrushchev-Kennedy summit meeting in 1960, which was aborted when a U2 spy aircraft was shot down while spying deep inside Soviet territory. I have personal

---

[86] Angela Tuckett, Ibid. p. 373.

recollections of the time of very heated arguments among the left-wing students at Aberdeen University, between communists who insisted that Khrushchev was perfectly justified in walking out of the summit when no American apology was forthcoming and those of us who believed the issues at stake were far too important to warrant such impulsive behaviour.

At the 1959 Conference of the Labour Party the CP's Cold War perspectives in this respect had significant consequences, and the actions of Scottish communists were centrally important when a 'Ban the Bomb' resolution was defeated, though this was overshadowed by the Clause IV dispute. The miners' vote ensured that it was, and it was the Scottish miners who swung the balance in the NUM delegation, much to Daly's disgust. A letter from the London party centre to the Scottish District Committee at the end of 1958, expressed in congratulatory terms, ' ... the party in Scotland is a model for other Districts to follow,' and exhorting the District to prepare for the expected general election the following year, yet it does not mention CND,[87] (admittedly it was in very early stages). The Scottish Committee Report to the District Congress in March the same year) leads with 'The Fight for Peace', asserting that 'The men who produced [the 1957 Defence White Paper] should be indicted for high treason or certified as lunatics', again ignoring any unilateralist demand and focuses on 'forcing Summit Talks'.[88] (A leaflet the party used under the title 'Ban the Bomb', 5000 distributed in Scotland, was intended in the context of summit negotiations, not a unilateralist one).

Nevertheless, when realisation dawned that large numbers of young communists were ignoring the party's official coldness towards CND and identifying themselves with the movement, the CP leaders were

---

[87] John Gollan to Scottish Committee, November 25 1958, CP Scottish Committee Archive, Glasgow Caledonian University.
[88] Communist Party Scottish Committee Political Report to Scottish Congress 1958, March 22 and 23. (Ibid.) A 'Discussion Statement' presented to this Congress opens with the statement that 'Every comrade can be proud of the work of our Party in Scotland in the past year. By collecting 50, 000 signatures on Peace Petitions ... '

pragmatic enough to alter their stance. By early 1960 it had become official CP policy to support CND, and its activists brought considerable organisational assistance to the Campaign. At the famous 1960 Labour Party Congress at Scarborough the Scottish miners played an opposite role from that of the previous year, and the unilateralist resolution was narrowly passed. The event, though spectacular, did not make much difference in the long run, for CND was not sufficiently embedded in the labour movement to hold on to its victory and the 1960 resolution was effectively reversed a year later.

Even when it had decided to throw in its lot with CND the party nevertheless continued to maintain its 'own' peace organisation which it had inherited from its years of isolation, the British Peace Committee – which even had its own youth section, the Youth Peace Committee, and a Scottish section as well, the Scottish Peace Committee. The BPC badges – a Picasso-style white dove on a blue background, were to be seen on the anti-nuclear marches beside the CND symbol – though in nothing like equivalent numbers. The Scottish Peace Committee gets only low-key mention, however, in the available Scottish CP documents.

Polaris

By the time that happened the focus of the anti-nuclear campaign had shifted to Scotland, with the establishment of a US nuclear submarine base at the Holy Loch beside Dunoon. Marches, sit-downs and inventive demonstrations involving small boats characterised the year following its appearance in 1961. The Scottish communists were in their element. In late 1960, in anticipation of the base's establishment, the STUC General Council was persuaded to issue a statement condemning the project and to lobby Scottish Labour parliamentarians to protest against it (they did not) and finally to organise a public protest in Glasgow in December 1960. Others were undertaken by trades councils in Paisley, Edinburgh, Dundee, Kirkcaldy, Cowdenbeath and the Vale of Leven, at some of which

Middleton was the principal speaker. By 1963 the STUC had firmly committed itself to unilateralism, including in its composite resolution the statement that:

> Congress opposes in every way the government's efforts in having an independent nuclear deterrent. It views with disgust this hideous investment in Polaris submarines by the Government whose only possible use is the massacre of workers and trade unionists in other lands.

Appropriately, the resolution was moved by Mick McGahey, Moffat's successor as the Scottish NUM President.[89]

The Scottish communists, however, were energetically active on the ground in the demonstrations as well as on the floor of trade union movement meetings, participating alongside the mass of demonstrators and enhancing their credibility. The songs composed for the anti-Polaris protests, unlike those heard on the regular CND marches, were witty, irreverent and demotic, some of them composed by songwriters who were also party members. And example is:

> Why do the Yanks look blue – Yuri Gagarin!
> Why are they number two – Yuri Gagarin!

This is a reference to the Soviet cosmonaut who made the first earth orbit in 1961. Probably the best known was, Ding Dong Dollar, sung to the tune of 'She'll be Comin' round the Mountain' and the chorus being:

> Oh, ye canna spend a dollar when ye're deid,
> Oh ye canna spend a dollar when ye're deid
> Singing ding dong dollar, everybody holler,
> Oh, ye canna spend a dollar when ye're deid!

---

[89] Tuckett, Ibid. pp. 374–9.

These verses were regarded as very funny at the time, though they would now, along with other anti-Polaris songs, be censured for political incorrectitude.

May Day 1952. Scottish Communists (Ruchill Branch) marching in Glasgow. *(Glasgow Caledonian University, Gallacher Memorial Library)*

Contact with the anti-nuclear movement revived the party, and it began to grow again, so that by the mid-sixties membership had recovered to the level prior to 1956. The fact that the Soviet bloc at this period was able to project itself regarding Cold War issues, on the whole, in a relatively favourable light, undoubtedly helped.

I was led to joining the Communist Party through my activity in the Peace Movement.

I was active in the Council for Nuclear Disarmament Branch in my area and marched in the demonstrations in Glasgow and the Holy Loch.

In the course of doing this I came into contact with members of the

Communist Party and it seemed to me that they had the best understanding of the nature of the world situation, the reason for the danger of war and how to prevent war.

This is why I joined ... [90]

And from the same document:

> One of the first things we did was to deputise the Local District Council on the question of the Polaris Base.
>
> We were delighted when they allowed us to speak to them and even more so when we learned that on the basis of our deputation the Council had decided to pass a resolution protesting against the establishment of this base in Scotland.[91]

At that time the Labour Party had a newly-founded youth organisation, the Young Socialists, and in Aberdeen for example, the branch was assiduously courted by the city's Young Communist League, which did indeed succeed in attracting a number of the YS members into its ranks.

Renewed Growth

It is not surprising that the Scottish communists (though they did a lot of other things as well) continued in the early sixties to play to this major strength. It is noted above that their 1958 Congress (not to be confused with the national all-British congresses, held in alternate years) did not take a unilateralist position – and this continued through 1959 – nevertheless highlighted international negotiations and the avoidance of nuclear war as the top priority. The 1960 Congress came just too early for the switch to supporting CND, at a time when the Khrushchev-Kennedy summit was in prospect, and again 'The Fight for Peace' led

---

[90] 'Extracts from the Political Report by Gordon McLennan, District Secretary', 1962 Congress Reporting Back Guide p. 3. Scottish Committee Archive.

the headings, the Scottish Committee congratulating itself for having sent 'a powerful contingent of 550 men and women.' to the CP demonstration for Peace and Independence in June 1958.[92]

Similarly, at the 1962 Congress 'The Fight for Peace' tops the agenda, with the Scottish Committee report declaring that:

Since our last Congress the development of the fight for peace has received the constant and increasing attention of the Scottish Committee and the Scottish party has played an outstanding role in the development of mass struggle on the peace issues.

Following our last Congress the Summit Conference which was to be held in May 1960 was sabotaged by the United States ... An intensive campaign was carried out by the Party at the factory gates and in the movement to explain the role of the United States government in sabotaging this conference.

In November 1960 we had the announcement by the Tory Government of their intention to give the United States permission to establish the Polaris submarine base on the Holy Loch. Our Party gave prompt and decisive leadership for the mobilisation of the Labour movement and the entire Scottish people against this proposal and helped to develop in Scotland a mighty movement which involved wide sections of the people.

As a result of this struggle all sections of the peace movement have grown and developed and tens of thousands of people have been brought into active struggle for peace for the first time.

Joint activity in the campaign against Polaris laid the basis for the development of further joint action of the peace movement against the threat of war and the work of all sections of the peace movement has grown steadily during this period.

The young people have made an outstanding contribution both in the fight against Polaris and more recently in the demonstration in Wales against the establishment of a German base there.

[91] Ibid.
[92] 'Report of the Work of the Scottish Committee covering the period January 1958–January 1960', Scottish Committee Archive.

A consistent campaign of explanation has been carried out by the Party in the last 12 months to warn the people of the menace of German militarism, and the need for a peaceful settlement of the Berlin and German problem. The distribution of leaflets dealing with this question, the organisation of many meetings, poster parades and discussions in Labour movement organisations, have helped to focus attention on this major issue.[93]

The separate 'Congress Discussion Statement' also highlighted and prioritised the 'Fight for Peace', concluding that section with the slogans, 'No War over Berlin – Negotiations Now! No German Bases in Scotland! Remove the Polaris Base from the Holy Loch!'[94] The Political Report – the keynote speech delivered by the Scottish Secretary, Gordon McLennan at the Congress, also begins with the theme of 'Peace', and in this he notes that, 'A new chapter of peace activity has now been opened up in Scotland ... now the campaign is under way for the Glasgow CND March on the last Saturday of this month ... '[95] Parliamentary election material reflected similar priorities. In June 1952 Gordon McLennan stood as the communist candidate in the West Lothian by-election against Tam Dalyell as the Labour candidate. McLennan's election address preliminary begins with the slogan:

Vote for Peace, against the Bomb – End British manufacture, testing and use of all nuclear weapons – Clear out Polaris and German troops – Negotiate an agreement now for world disarmament.'

and the text proper starts with the paragraph:

No worker in West Lothian can doubt that continued Tory rule will bring disaster to Britain. We must end the nuclear arms race and secure

---

[93] Report of the Scottish Committee, Covering the Period January 1960 to January 1962, Scottish District Congress, 17–18 March 1962. Ibid.
[94] This was the only section of the Statement to have slogans attached to it.
[95] 'Extracts', p. 1.

the destruction of all nuclear weapons. Unless this is done we live on the edge of a terrible nuclear war, either by accident or design. In such a war our country would face deadly peril ... Alone of all the candidates in this by-election I stand for a policy that will guarantee peace for us and our children and make Britain safe for future generations.

Ironically, in view of Tam Dalyell's later role in the Labour Party, he accused Dalyell of having a dubious political background, i.e. he had been a Tory, a Gaitskellite and a supporter of Britain's nuclear role.

Clearly these campaigns, together with others on trade union and social questions. were not without their effect. Membership, at 6,451 by 1962, had risen to over 1,000 more than at the previous Congress and in local elections gains outweighed losses, giving a total of thirteen communist councillors in Scotland. On the other hand, even by the time this congress took place, CND was in steep decline and this very valuable recruiting base for the party was diminishing rapidly. (The Vietnam campaign, soon to follow, though it had various positive effects for the party and led to recruitment in some areas, did not result in overall numerical growth). By the time of the 1964 Congress ('Peace' was once again the principal heading) membership had risen even further, to 7,761[96] which was more or less its upper limit.

Of course the CPGB was unable, any more than anyone in Britain (probably not even the Prime Minister) to exercise any influence on the Cuban missile crisis of October 1962, when the worst fears of the anti-nuclear movement came close to being realised. That was shortly followed, however, by the Test Ban Treaty and an easing of the perils of nuclear confrontation until Ronald Reagan revived them in the 1980s.

---

[96] 'Report of the Scottish Committee Covering the Period January 1962 to June 1964', Scottish Congress, 22 November 1964. Scottish Committee Archive. There were also 1,334 enrolled in the Young Communist League in Scotland, with a substantial, though not complete, overlapping membership.

Conclusion

That the CPGB identified itself with the Soviet position in the Cold War is not in dispute, and its members were not ashamed of the fact. They did so because they believed, misguidedly or not, that the Soviet Bloc represented peace and progress and the Western powers, war and reaction, that the US postures were aggressive and the Soviet side was exercising legitimate self-defence – a position satirised in the song sung by the neo-Trotskyists of the International Socialists (later the Socialist Workers Party), 'The Workers' Bomb'. Even as party members fraternised and collaborated with CND activists they never failed to insist that the blame for the threat lay with the United States and its British political allies.[97]

The party, however, was not mistaken in identifying concern at the possibility of nuclear Armageddon, while stocks of 'the ultimate weapon' multiplied on both sides, as a source of great unease among the general public; and after some false starts, succeeded in connecting itself with this sentiment and making that its priority. The emphasis served it well, for by 1964 it had recovered numerically to where it had been in 1956, and, sadder and wiser, was in some ways better placed to intervene in the crises of Harold Wilson's premiership than it would have been without the disasters of the mid-fifties. These considerations appear to have applied particularly in Scotland, where by 1964 the CP had assumed the postures of a dynamic and self-confident organisation, convinced that it was on the verge of a breakthrough in growth and electoral advance.

Although these hopes were soon disappointed, there were compensations. By that time the STUC agenda on international issues coincided with those of the party.[98] Throughout the sixties the CP was very influential in the STUC and in 1976 the STUC elected a communist General Secretary, Jimmy Milne. Party influence in the trade

---

[97] For example, in a pamphlet entitled *Who is to Blame?*
[98] It avoided a damaging and probably terminal split over the Warsaw Pact invasion of Czechoslovakia in 1968 by condemning it.

union movement grew for two decades despite the disgrace of the ETU ballot-rigging trial in 1961 (though that left permanent scars), and nowhere more so than in Scotland.

Of course it would be absurd to attribute this solely to the position it took up and the activity it carried out on the issues of the Cold War

between 1960 and 1962. There were many other considerations influencing its relative success during those years. Nevertheless, the presumptions which induced it to put 'Peace' always at the head of its programmatic documents were not misplaced. That not only fitted with its members' sentiments, but enabled the party to climb out of the discredit into which it had been pushed in the earlier phases of the Cold War.

May Day 1952: Scottish Communists (Govanhill Branch) marching in Glasgow. *(Glasgow Caledonian University, Gallacher Memorial Library)*

Author Unknown. A message for the public and the Ministry of Defence. *(© Brian P Jamison)*

Chapter 3

COLD WAR PSYCHOHISTORY IN THE SCOTTISH PSYCHE

Alastair McIntosh

The Inner Life of Conflict

It is customary to think of the Cold War as having been a post-Second World War phenomenon, tersely strung between Stalin and Gorbachev. Whilst that may be so within a narrowly defined system boundary, it is psychologically naïve. To appreciate the wider and deeper perspective, we must inform our discourse with psychohistory – the emerging discipline that examines inter-relationships between 'outer' or 'factual' historical events and the 'inner' and 'mythic' psychodynamic processes of individuals and whole peoples. Without such a challenging approach, it is impossible adequately to address either the aetiology or the prognosis of Scotland's ongoing Cold War.

Superficially, the Cold War was about an East-West standoff – communism versus capitalism conceived very much in 20th century terms. However, I want to suggest that, psychologically speaking, this was just a presenting symptom of a much larger syndrome of modernity; one deeply embedded in a need dualistically to draw a line and distinguish an in-group from an out-group. I have lost count of how many times I have heard senior military officers privately say, 'When we joined the Services it was clear cut. The Russians were over there, we were over here, and our job was to keep it that way. But since the Berlin Wall came down, we're not so sure where the line is drawn and for what we may be asked to fight.'

Post-9/11, that line has, in many minds, been reconsolidated. The enemy that was 'communism' is now 'terrorism'. 'He' is now

Arabic/Islamic rather than Red. He comes replete with a latter-day highly-personalised demonology of Bin Laden, Saddam and other Tarot-esque gamblers (or gambled with) on fate's deck of cards. This transmogrification of one enemy into another was psychologically inevitable. The Berlin Wall came down in outer history, yet the inner structures that had sustained it remained in place. Those controlling power in the West spoke of the 'Peace Dividend' outwardly, but overlooked the inner need to adjust to events. They failed to see the authoritarian mind's need to see the world in simple, black and white terms, and if necessary to manufacture such seemingly-secure polarities to maintain group identity and purpose (Pennington, Gillen & Hill, 1999; Gromyko & Hellman, 1988).

In my experience, notwithstanding their interest in 'psyops' (psychological operations), many of the military (and politicians) are considerably resistant to examining their own relationship to psychodynamics. Arguably, for some, and, perhaps, for these subcultures as a generalisation, it brings home too many unresolved issues from alienated and alienating early childhoods where, as has been widely biographically demonstrated with many key figures, strong team and leadership identity has seemingly emerged from a fractured primal integrity (Duffell 2000; Miller 1987; Gillegan 1997; McIntosh 2001). It is true that there has been recent CIA interest in the disturbed childhood psychodynamics of figures like Saddam Hussein, particularly through the work of Dr Jerrold Post (Borger 2002), but I have also heard the significance of this played down within the military, perhaps with some immediate tactical justification, as 'lacking sufficiently reliable predictive power'. I wish to emphasise that, in drawing attention to the psychopathology of war, it is crucial not to overplay the hand and pathologise away real threat. My appeal to integrating psychodynamic insight with objectively factual history is not to deny the very real issues upon which conflict can be pegged – for example, the human rights record of the former Soviet Union, offensive military build-ups, Saddam's gassing of the Kurds, the West's greed for oil, a festering Israel/Palestine situation, Crusade interwoven with Jihad in the minds of militant fundamentalists on both sides, and so on. These realities are of great importance. Rather, I am highlighting the need to remember that consciousness is a function of outer perception and inner cognition. We must therefore try to 'read' geopolitics with eyes less tinted by projections. Equally, we must learn, as one of the arts of peace, how to de-couple the other's projections (and, in psychodynamic parlance, countertransferences) onto us. Achieving such mutually clear recognition between peoples and in their representatives is prerequisite to avoiding the continual generation of new enemies. Without such psychological awareness, any remaining Peace Dividend from the Cold War is doomed to improvidence, and perhaps catastrophically so.

Dynamics of the Split Psyche

My position is well summed up by the Indian Jesuit thinker, Anthony de Mello. 'Do you know where wars come from?' he asks. 'They come from projecting outside of us the conflict that is inside. Show me an individual in whom there is no inner self-conflict and I'll show you an individual in whom there is no violence' (de Mello, 1992, 182).

Applying this to Cold War psychohistory means exploring beyond the geopolitical, military and economic, presenting symptoms and examining possible applications of analytical (which is to say, Jungian) depth psychology. As a contemporary Jungian political thinker puts it, 'What connects depth psychology and politics is a preoccupation with therapy. The analyst of complexes is preoccupied with the therapy of the individual; the analyst of politics is preoccupied with the therapy of the nation or society or the world' (Samuels, 1993, 30).

What, then, might be a framework for such analysis?

Whilst aspects of Freudian theory have been discredited in recent years, few would challenge Freud's basic observation that conflict between inner needs and the outer socially-imposed 'reality principle' may be reduced by a process of splitting off from ego-consciousness, and repression into the personal unconscious. 'Go, go, go, said the bird,' in Eliot's Four Quartets, 'human kind/ Cannot bear very much reality.'

In Freud's understanding, civilisation emerges out of sublimated dissonance between the urge for pleasure, and the 'reality principle' of social norms that constrain it (Freud 1991; Brown 1991).

Jung further developed this into what he called 'complex psychology' – the psychology of the quasi-autonomous 'complexes' that result from splitting parts off from conscious awareness. He introduced the term, 'complex', (first used by Bleuler), or 'feeling-toned complex', to designate 'groups of feeling-toned ideas in the unconscious' (Jacobi 1968, 36–39). A suitable analogy is an electromagnetic field, 'toned', or given distinctively tuned characteristics, by specific magnetic disturbances. Here, the 'magnetic disturbances' are traumatic or uncomfortable emotional circumstances, and the 'electromagnetic field' is the 'libido' – the energy of the psyche. 'Psyche', in turn, can be defined as the totality of what it means to be a human being, 'body, mind and soul'. In Jung's view, psyche is ultimately interconnected with the rest of reality; with the totality of human and all other nature. He therefore surmised: 'People who know nothing about nature are of course neurotic, for they are not adapted to reality' (Jung 1967, 190).

To Jung, then, ordinary psychic 'dis-ease' or neurosis resulted from a defective adjustment to reality. It is as if the energy-charged complexes keep knocking on life's door, reminding that not all is well within. More radical psychic disease – psychosis – arises when complexes don't merely tap on the ego's carefully controlled constructs of conscious life, but start to take it over. Jung saw war in these terms. He saw the Second World War as an outbreak of collective psychosis rooted in overly-rational modern humankind's alienation from mythic and erotic expression.

Those unacceptable and denied parts which have been split off from the conscious life of the psyche contribute to what Jung called the 'shadow' – Dr Jekyll's alter-ego in Mr Hyde. The problem is not that we all have psychological shadows. It is that when we deny the constellation of repressed complexes that make up our shadow, the psyche seems to have a peculiar talent for projecting it out into the world in ways that we don't always realise. It is as if the hidden inner world shapes our outer perceptual and cognitive frameworks. Our capacity to see is constrained by what we are, and inasmuch as we don't understand what we are, so much the worse for us and those around us. The 'other', who we demonise, may say more about ourselves than about them. It is as if we have an inclination to most hate in others that which has been hermetically compartmentalised and repressed with an inner violence within ourselves. Thus, for example, the gay-basher may be the upright and uptight pillar of the establishment who most fears his own latent homosexuality. The pacifist may be adept at passive-aggression, and so on. The individual least grounded in her own cultural identity may be the one who most yearns the acceptance of in-group solidarity by stirring hatred against out-groups – as with the woman who was convicted a few years ago for putting up anti-English 'Settler Watch' notices in the Scottish Highlands, and was a German incomer!

Applied militarily, mechanisms of splitting, repression and projection force us to ask how far our fears of the other really are justified. How much does our perception of the misdeeds of the 'enemy' differ from their perception of ours? Studies of the social psychology of prejudice and stereotyping demonstrate how very easy it is to cultivate a group dynamic of misrepresentation and hatred. Sometimes, this may be justified – there being good reason to fear the other. 'Just because you're paranoid doesn't mean they're not out to get you.' Other times, we may be adding fuel to the fire because we have perhaps justifiably erected outward defences, but failed to attend to our own inner constellation of forces that influences the assessment of threat. To invert the popular expression, 'Just because they're out to get you doesn't mean you're not paranoid.'

We can probably say that any situation where there is a clear-cut 'us-and-them' dynamic, together with caricature to a mythological degree, is conducive of shadow projection. Both the Cold War and the current War on Terrorism unmistakably show these features. Saddam was a 'monster', no doubt, but as former Labour Party minister Denis Healey said at the onset of the First Gulf War, 'he's a monster [in part] of our own making.' Add to this the power of stereotyping in group roles, and the hypnotic power of obedience to authority, and it becomes indisputable that very little stands between an otherwise nice person and the capacity severely to abuse others (Haney, Banks & Zimbardo 1973; Milgram 1974). Cold War 'Reds under the beds' psychology is a disturbingly everyday psychopathology ... and by the way ... notice the revealing psychodynamic allusion in that expression – precisely why, we might ask, should it be our 'beds' that the 'Reds' ostensibly lurk 'under'?

Splitting of the Psyche and Atoms

In psychological terms, then, the Cold War can be seen as a splitting of the entire world into a charged polarity. In its late-modern form, this took place in a context of Stalinist pogroms on the one hand, and McCarthyite fascism on the other. Each of these rendered the occupation of intellectual and ontological middle ground unsafe, thereby focussing energy at the extremes. Each sought total obedience to its own way of relating to reality and was, as such, both neurotic and totalitarian; in sum, like the iconic Dr Strangelove, they were psychotic. Each necessitated a psychic splitting and repression in the collective unconscious. It then took either enormous courage to refuse to conform, or self-breaking of the spirit to toe the party line and, in so doing, offend against inner integrity. When such a collective wounded self was projected back out onto the other, the consequences in military firepower were globally life threatening.

The main presenting symptom of the Cold War was a conflict between the command economic paradigm, and the market economy. In both, economy is a proxy for power. The impact of this on human life ought not be underestimated. As Lady Thatcher put it in May 1988, 'Economics are the method. The object is to change the soul' (in Roberts 2002, 300). The command-market polarity may therefore be seen as being about much more than how the groceries are delivered. Arguably, it parallels the axiomatic Freudian dichotomy between the pleasure and reality principles. To the Soviets (and, for that matter, the Chinese), the West was 'decadent'. Equally, to the West, the Soviets were 'Godless', which amounts to much the same stereotypical projection. Each, at the extremes, saw the other as inhuman – mad and bad. Each system of political economy, inasmuch as it operated as a system of domination rather than of empowerment, was, in its own way, unreal, inhumane and unsustainable. As such, the Cold War represented a contest over 'civilisation' itself. Both sides equally feared the savage wildness that might break out if the walls of their particular worldview were breached: '… they were over there, we were over here, and our job was to keep it that way.'

Notwithstanding Europe's decreasingly audible lip-service to a mixed economy, neither side could see an authentic third or middle way. It was not just the old-style Soviets who felt their peace troubled when the Berlin Wall came down. The entire East-West dysfunctional co-dependency became destabilised. Public attention had consternated itself with the energy that might be released from malevolently splitting the atom. Most did not realise that the whole show, actually, was constellated by the libidinal energy fission of a split in the collective psyche. Apartheid was not just a concept applicable to South Africa, and radiotoxicity penetrated the mind with omega emissions – intimations of end times, so to speak – beyond merely the physicist's alpha, beta and gamma.

Scotland's Cold War – Culloden to 9/11

In Scotland we have a peculiar saying about matters that we know to be of dysfunctional intergenerational cultural consequence. We'll often say, 'It all goes back to Culloden.'

The Battle of Culloden near Inverness in 1746 was, as can be testified by the many who recall it like yesterday, our 'Road to Basra' experience of total military humiliation. It was the last battle ever staged on mainland British soil. It represented the final consolidation of the nascent British state in the wake of the Union of the Crowns (1603), and the massively unpopular Acts of Union (1707). These had the effect of forging England and Scotland into one 'United Kingdom of Great Britain'. When, in 1745, Scots Jacobites under Prince Charles Edward Stuart rose up and marched on London, they were subsequently neutralised at Culloden (by forces drawn from both England and Scotland). Thereafter, with the British state internally secure against Scots alliances with the French, the British Empire was free to expand. But what was the psychological cost of such imperialism?

Robert Burns, Scotland's national bard, wrote his iconic two-verse Strathallan's Lament in 1767, just twenty-one years after Culloden. In this poem he stands in the shoes of the 5th Viscount Strathallan, whose father had been slain by the battle's vanquishing troops.

Burns portrays an old world order replaced by an emotionally vacant brave new world; one in which neither the wild beauty of nature nor the soft conviviality of human community (the 'busy haunts of base mankind') can any longer give solace. The young Strathallan's very capacity for perception is altered. No longer can he see his world as before.

> Thickest night, surround my dwelling!
> Howling tempests, o'er me rave!
> Turbid torrents wintry-swelling,
> Roaring by my lonely cave!
> Crystal streamlets gently flowing,
> Busy haunts of base mankind,
> Western breezes softly blowing,
> Suit not my distracted mind.
>
> In the cause of Right engaged,
> Wrongs injurious to redress,
> Honour's war we strongly waged,
> But the heavens deny'd success.
> Ruin's wheel has driven o'er us;
> Not a hope that dare attend,
> The wide world is all before us,
> But a world without a friend.

(in Mackay 1993, 287)

From a Scottish point of view, those last two lines arguably sum up the whole primal aetiology of the Cold War. As I have shown elsewhere (McIntosh 2001), Burns was not alone amongst his contemporaries in making this diagnosis. Neither is this the only Burnsian output to pinpoint such decisive cause. Indeed, probably the reason why Burns is our national bard is his capacity to minister so astutely to the soul of nationhood.

From Culloden onwards, Scotland was forced to adopt the role of Anglo-American adjutant in Empire. The landed and mercantile classes spawned a breed of 'Enlightenment' or 'imperial Scots' such as Adam Smith, and the perceived barbarism, once projected onto Gaelic Scots and Irish people as the alien 'other' during the reign of James VI & I, became re-projected onto dark-skinned peoples in the colonies. The Scots psyche was left fissured by colonial violence. On the one hand, it championed imperialism; on the other, internationalism. For example, in 'Exterminate all the Brutes', the Swedish writer, Sven Lindqvist, notes that the founding figure behind 'scientific racism' was an Edinburgh University professor of anatomy, Robert Hooke – also of Burke and Hare body-snatching fame. In polar contrast, Lindqvist points out that it was another Scot, R. B. Cunninghame Graham, who became one of the few effective 19th century voices to urge the emancipation of colonised peoples (Lindqvist 2002; see also Fraser 2002). On the one hand, then, Knox was teaching the inferiority of blacks and maintaining, 'the only real right is physical force … laws are made to bind the weak, to be broken by the strong.' On the other, Cunninghame Graham became Joseph Conrad's closest friend and helped to inspire his Heart of Darkness analysis of colonialism; an analysis which, consistent with the psychology posited in this paper, suggested that 'darkest Africa' is, in reality, a projection of the West's own dark heart (Lindqvist 2002).

Set in the psychohistorical context, the Cold War is nothing new to Scotland. It is merely the ongoing desiccating blast of a 'world without a friend'; a world that Scotland was pushed into, part-willingly, part-kicking, as the 'divide and rule' tactic of British internal consolidation first split, and then yoked the opposites of so-called 'Caledonian

Antisyzgy', into Scotland's chariot as the Queen's-owned first lieutenant of Empire. In the driving seat has been a 'might is right' presumption of God-given 'manifest destiny' to plunder a post-Edenic 'fallen' world, first through overt global colonisation and now, with her one-time American scion, through globalisation's market domination.

The supporting cast includes both modern weapons, and modern marketing techniques. Each explodes in consciousness with surgical precision, distorting perception as to what constitutes 'right' or proportional relationship with one another and with the planet. Indeed, it is apposite to observe that marketing, as a discipline, only fully emerged after the Second World War. American corporations in particular feared losing the market share they had built up under a war economy. The 'Depth Boys' school of motivational manipulation was employed by leading corporations to turn the therapeutic insights of Freud, Jung and Adler, linked to the behavioural psychology of Pavlov and Skinner, towards baiting emotional triggers that would 'hook' into addictive, newly invented 'needs' (Packard 1960; Sheth, Mittal & Newman 1999).

And as Burns saw with a compassionate eye, it set in process a Molochean 'world without a friend'.

This is what makes it all so 'cold', and why it is a matter of 'war'. This is why the Cold War neither started with Stalin, nor ended with Gorbachev; and why its aetiology and prognosis should be of the utmost concern to Scots and other sentient beings.

Towards a Cultural Psychotherapy

Today, post-Berlin Wall, fresh geopolitical tension related to globalisation culminated in the World Trade Towers being the focus of the attacks of 9/11. As was to be expected, the Cold War has 'hotted up' again, the dividing line re-projected as an 'Axis of Evil'. We might note, in passing, the dualistic rhetoric from America that 'if you're not with us, you're against us.' We might note, too, Donald Rumsfeld's effort to polarise Europe into 'Old' and 'New', and we might question whether

America really thinks there is room in the world for the newly-minted Euro to rival the dollar as a potentially alternative petro currency.

We might further note that the Islamic world, following years of civic distortion by oil-bloated semi-puppet dictatorships left by former colonial powers, has become tinder-dry to reciprocate its own shadow projection onto the West. Furthermore, it has found a constellating righteous cause in the complex that has, since Biblical times, become the Israel-Palestine altercation. Meanwhile, Islamic economics, with its carefully thought-through critique of usury, happens to be one of the few significant intellectual challenges potentially capable of troubling advanced capitalism (Choudhury & Malik 1992; Visser & McIntosh 1998). Indeed, I have argued, elsewhere, that the Islamic critique of capitalism, because of its implications for Discounted Cash Flow investment appraisal methodology, may be one of the deepest fault lines in the psyche of our times (McIntosh 2004, at press).

Psychologically, it has been clear even from before the First Gulf War that we live in Tolkeinesque archetypal times. The world's 'dark lords' are dragging us all into a slow Armageddon as they play out 'final showdowns' (and not just in the movies) between 'good and evil', emanating, arguably, in considerable measure, from schizoid splits in their own unexamined inner lives and class subcultures.

The real battle – the battle to become self-aware – the battle to expose and understand the 'myth of redemptive violence' (Wink 1992) – is not as easy as sitting in an armchair setting off fire-and-forget weapons. If we want to live in a different world, we must start by getting real about the state we are in. We must get to grips with the repressed historical complexes that have been driving us to collective schizophrenia led by rather too many iceman psychopaths. We must consider the need for cultural psychotherapies.

In personal psychotherapy, an individual is helped to recover his repressed history, so that he understands how his being has been constructed, and perhaps distorted and stunted. A similar process maybe needs to happen with the soul of nations. We need to recover those parts of our shared national histories that have been kept off the curriculum, and see how they have shaped us as peoples.

This means understanding not only factual history, but also the story of the cultural soul. We can do this helped by such post-colonial writers as Paulo Freire, Alice Walker, Frantz Fanon, bel hooks, Gustavo Gutiérrez, Adrienne Rich, Ben Okri, Starhawk and Hugh MacDiarmid – yes, there are plenty of them, and that's just for starters.

We need to create contexts to explore how we feel about our history and not just what we think of it. The arts are crucial in this. We need to recognise that there are parts of us, collectively, that have developed in distorted ways, parts that are stunted, and maybe some parts that have never developed at all. It's about getting behind the emotionally frozen stiff upper lip, and beyond.

In Scotland, we have already been experimenting with this in reclaiming Highland Clearance history, exploring the emotionally cauterising knock-on effects of intergenerational trauma (Hunter 1995; Newton 2000; McIntosh 2001). The political consciousness raised by such popular education contributed hugely towards the passing in 2003 of the Land Reform (Scotland) Act. We now need to extend such profound reflection to other areas of life and, especially, to our relationship with violence. We need to understand the processes of conflict recognition, reconciliation and forgiveness – as, for example, are pointed towards by South Africa's Truth and Reconciliation Commission, and by a growing number of other instances where principles of non-violence have been applied to considerable positive political effect (Johnston & Sampson 1994; Wink 1992).

We can do this work all the more powerfully if we do it jointly with those we have misunderstood and hurt in the past – for example, with the Irish, with East Europeans, with people of colour, and with our Muslim sisters and brothers.

We can make such healing of nationhood part of creating an ethnically inclusive Scottish national identity – moving towards Scots internationalism in a co-operative 'One World' ethos that gradually replaces the competitive paradigm of globalisation. And of course, what is said for Scotland here, and Scotland's Cold War, could apply to many other nations – England and the US too.

We can embody this in our trade relations, such as buying organic and 'Fair Trade' products where we can, and in generally seeking to live in accordance with social justice and environmental sustainability. After all, corporations are responsible for structural injustices only in part, because their greed is also the projection of our aggregated individual mindless consumerism and investment policies. We cannot apportion blame without looking into mirrors. True, we will be confused by tricks with mirrors, but let that not excuse evasion from the imperative of facing up to reflections of our own dark shadows.

The wonderful and liberating irony of so doing, is that it is only possible in the light, and with eyes that have opened to seeing the light of interconnected human relationship. A wide world is, indeed, all before us. It need not remain devoid of friends.

REFERENCES

Borger, Julian (2002), 'Saddam, tell me about your mum', *The Guardian*, 14 November, www.guardian.co.uk, consulted 2-8-03 (NB. There is also a *Journal of Psychohistory* dedicated to this field – www.psychohistory.com – the articles in it seem to be of variable scholarly standard).

Brown, J. A. C. (1991), *Freud and the Post-Freudians*: London, Penguin.

Choudhury, M. A. and Malik, U. A. (1992) *The Foundations of Islamic Political Economy*, London: Macmillan.

de Mello, Anthony (1992), *Awareness: the perils and opportunities of Reality*: New York, Image Doubleday.

Duffell, Nick (2000), *The Making of Them: The British Attitude to Children and the Boarding School System:* London, Lone Arrow Press.

Fraser, Ian M. (2002). *R. B Cunninghame Graham – Fighter for Justice*: Gargunnock, privately printed.

Freud, Sigmund (1991), *On Metapsychology* (C.W. Vol. 11): London, Penguin.

Gilligan, James (1997), *Violence: Reflections on a National Epidemic*: New York, Vintage.

Gromyko, Anatoly & Hellman, Martin (eds.) (1988), *Breakthrough: Soviet and Western Scholars Issue a Challenge to Build a World Beyond War*: New York, Walker and Company.

Haney, C., Banks, C., & Zimbardo, P. (1973), 'Interpersonal Dynamics in a Simulated Prison', International Journal of Criminology and Penology, 1, 69-97.

Hunter, James (1995), *On the Other Side of Sorrow: Nature and People in the Scottish Highlands*: Edinburgh, Mainstream.

Jacobi, Jolande (1968), *The Psychology of C. G. Jung*: London, Routledge & Kegan Paul.

Johnston, Douglas & Sampson, Cynthia (eds.) (1994), *Religion, the Missing Dimension of*

Statecraft: Oxford, Oxford University Press.

Jung, Carl Gustav (1967), *Memories, Dreams, Reflections*: London, Fontana.

Lindqvist, Sven (2002), 'Exterminate all the Brutes': London, Granta.

Mackay, James A. (ed.) (2002), *Robert Burns: the Complete Poetical Works*: Darvel, Alloway Publishing.

McIntosh, Alastair (2001), *Soil and Soul: People versus Corporate Power*: London, Aurum Press.

McIntosh, Alastair (2004, at press), 'Foreword' to Europe, Globalisation and the Challenge of Sustainability, (ed, Brian Baxter et al.): London, Routledge, due February, ISBN: 0-415-30276-5.

Milgram, Stanley (1974), *Obedience to Authority*: London, Tavistock.

Miller, Alice (1987), *For Your Own Good: The Roots of Violence in Child-rearing*: London, Virago.

Newton, Michael (2000), *A Handbook of the Scottish Gaelic World*: Dublin, Four Courts Press.

Packard, Vance (1960), *The Hidden Persuaders*: Harmondsworth, Penguin.

Pennington, Donald, Gillen, Kate & Hill, Pam (1999), *Social Psychology*: London, Arnold.

Roberts, Richard (2002), *Religion, Theology and the Human Sciences, Cambridge*: Cambridge University Press.

Samuels, Andrew (1993), *The Political Psyche*: London, Routledge.

Sheth, Jagdish N., Mittal, Banwari & Newman, Bruce I. (1999), *Customer Behavior: Consumer Behaviour and Beyond*: Fort Worth, Dryden Press.Visser,

Wayne & McIntosh, Alastair (1998), 'An evaluation of the historical condemnation of usury', *Accounting, Business & Financial History*, Vol. 8:2, 175–189.

Wink, Walter (1992), *Engaging the Powers: Discernment and Resistance in a World of Domination*: Philadelphia, Fortress Press.

Chapter 5

JUNIOR MILITARY COMMAND DURING THE COLD WAR

Major (Retired) Alastair Campbell
Argyll and Sutherland Highlanders

This submission is based on my own experiences as an officer in the Argyll and Sutherland Highlanders in the period 1972–1996, and subsequent employment as a Ministry of Defence civil servant. The remarks made here are entirely my own and should not in any way be construed as official comment from the Ministry of Defence nor even as representing the views of my own regiment. Throughout most of this period the principal 'raison d'être' of military service was to counter what we perceived to be the expansionist ambitions of Communism in general and the Soviet Union in particular.

Any discussion on the Cold War and its impact on Scotland requires a military viewpoint. The term 'war' is used in the title, and therefore it is, by definition, a military matter. My specific experience consists of four tours in Germany, where NATO planned to fight the forward defensive battle of Western Europe in the event of attack by the Warsaw Pact armies. I was based in Osnabruck in the mid 1970s as a platoon commander, responsible for about thirty men, the most junior officer command. Subsequently, I became a Staff Officer in the Headquarters of the 1st Armoured Division, and was then a Company Commander (commanding approximately 120 men) in the 1st Battalion whilst based in Colchester. Despite being based in the UK our primary role was the reinforcement of British Forces in Germany in time of conflict. Finally, I was the Battalion Second in Command in Minden from 1990–92, after the collapse of the Berlin Wall and the dismantling of the Inner German Border.

The military experience of the Cold War was primarily based in West Germany where there has been a large British Garrison since the end of the War. However, it is smaller now than it has ever been, following the military cuts and 'Peace Dividend' of 'Options For Change' started in the early 1990s. Because the Argyll and Sutherland Highlanders are a part of the British Army, and not a purely Scottish force, what follows is a comment on a Scottish regiment's experience but in the wider British context.

Historical Perspective

Although no battalion of the Argyll and Sutherland Highlanders went into Normandy on D Day, three battalions followed up quickly afterwards. The 7th Battalion, composed largely of men from the Stirling, Falkirk and Grangemouth areas, landed on 11 June 1944. The 2nd Battalion landed on 21 June 1944 whilst on the same day, and a little further down the coast, the leading elements of the 5th (anti-tank) Battalion were landed. The 8th Battalion of the Regiment was approaching from the south, through Italy, and ended the war in Austria. Whilst the Allied armies were marching on Berlin from the West the Soviets were moving into Central Europe from the East. The 8th Battalion in Austria, in May 1945, was involved in one of the first interactions with the Russians. It had been made responsible for disarming and guarding the White Russian Cossack Division which had fought with Hitler against the Russians. The Cossacks, always anti-Soviet in sympathy, had moved en masse, with families and livestock, when the Germans had overrun the Caucasus and Ukraine. Thus the Division consisted of 15,000 men, 4,000 women, 2,500 children, 5,000 horses and twelve dromedaries! The liaison officer with the Cossacks was a Major Davies who wrote at the time:

My responsibility is to try and get them to carry out British orders – not an easy task, because although the officers were willing to help, the discipline of the division was conspicuous only by its absence. In June orders were received to send all the Cossacks back to Russia, which was the fate they had been dreading, and consequently there was considerable unrest and desertion. As the camps were neither wired nor guarded it was not difficult to escape into the mountains, as many did, but it did not simplify the Battalion's duty of entraining them. After some unpleasant days this duty was completed.

Subsequent revelations of the nature of these unpleasant duties are a story in themselves. The 2nd Battalion remained in Europe until December 1946 when it returned to Colchester. Battalions of the Regiment were, therefore, present at the start of the occupation of mainland Europe, and were involved in the earliest events of the Cold War.

The hostility and distrust between Stalin on one side, and Churchill and Roosevelt on the other, were reflected in all contacts between Russian and Allied military personnel and had begun after D day. An Argyll officer, Ian Stonor, who had been captured by the Japanese trying to flee Singapore was eventually imprisoned in Manchuria, and liberated by the Russians in 1945. He recalled seeing Russian soldiers slashing the tyres of American aircraft, supposedly their allies, in order to slow their advance. He wrote afterwards: '… the ambitions of Soviet expansionism were evident to all who saw them, even then.' This is perhaps a little strong, but it is clear that the Cold War, the beginning of which is undefined, had started before the 'hot' Second World War had ended.

In 1948, postwar military reforms amalgamated the 1st and 2nd Battalions of the Regiment into one Battalion. It remained in Colchester until sent to Hong Kong in July 1949.

At 4 a.m. on Sunday 25 June 1950 a strong and well-trained North Korean Army, encouraged and supported by the Soviet Union, invaded South Korea and immediately overran all her forward defences. As a result of a plea by the United Nations Security Council on 27 June to 'furnish such assistance to the Republic of Korea as may be necessary to repel the armed attack and to restore international peace and security,' Britain decided to send troops. Allegedly, the same day, the British Cabinet met and committed Britain to the armed support of The Republic of Korea. As the meeting dispersed one of the secretaries said to the Prime Minister, Mr Attlee:

'Korea is rather a distant obligation Prime Minister.'

'Distant – yes,' Mr Attlee replied, 'but nonetheless an obligation.'[1]

And so it was that on Friday 25 August 1950, HQ 27 Brigade, which included the 1st Battalion of the Argyll and Sutherland Highlanders sailed out of Hong Kong for service under the United Nations flag. Some nine months later the Argylls returned to Hong Kong having lost thirty-one who were either killed in action or died of wounds, 165 were wounded and three were missing. Major Kenneth Muir was awarded the VC posthumously. The British total for this conflict was 1,078 British servicemen killed and 2,404 wounded. This was the price to be paid for 'a distant obligation – honourably discharged.' War by proxy, a feature of the Cold war, between Capitalism and Communism, had begun. And the regiment was the first British unit to take part in War by proxy.

This Battalion continued to play its part in the Cold War. Postings to Germany were frequent, and included Berlin twice, Lemgo, Osnabruck and Minden. When not in Germany the principal role of the Battalion was as a reinforcement for operations in Germany in the event of a Warsaw Pact invasion. Training throughout most of my service was focused largely on the Warsaw Pact and its capabilities. We were able to recount, almost parrot fashion, Soviet military principles, and identify many different vehicles and aircraft of the Soviet forces. Years later when the unification of East and West Germany occurred we were based in Minden. My house was close to the German Armed Forces Helicopter

---

[1] *The Official History: The British Part in the Korean War*, Vol 1-A. 'Distant Obligation, Anthony Farrar-Hockley, p. 33. HMSO 1990.

Pilots School. It was extremely disconcerting to see Soviet helicopters, with East German markings, which had only a short time before been the enemy, landing so close. A year or two earlier such a sight would have indicated that World War Three had begun.

The Warsaw Pact, and specifically the Soviet Union, was considered the enemy. Unauthorised fraternisation of any form was discouraged, even though the opportunities were few and restricted to a few formal contacts in and around Berlin.

Cold War Definition

What was the Cold War? 'Cold' and 'War' are a contradiction in terms.

Wars are traditionally described as 'hot'. However, although there are numerous books and endless references to the Cold War, definitions of it are few. When questioned, those asked provide answers which lead one to suspect that although they couldn't describe it, they knew it when they saw it.

The East German guard-changing took place daily at the Tomb of the Unknown Warrior in East Berlin. Note that the East Germans retained the 'goose step' marching style abandoned by the West German Armed Forces.
(Museum of the Argyll and Sutherland Highlanders)

It was a clash of ideologies by two principal powers, neither strong enough nor bold enough to attempt a pre-emptive attack and defeat the other. The Cold War was more than just a war - it was a conflict of many aspects. It was a conflict of politics, a conflict of media as well as a military one. Wars between the two main protagonists of the USA and the USSR were fought by proxy, as events showed in Korea, Vietnam and Angola, to name but three. The war was carried to other events, such as the Olympic Games and to the World Chess Championships. Whatever the War was, or was not, it had a profound effect on the lives of millions of people.

Warsaw Pact

The Warsaw Pact, formally known as the Warsaw Treaty of Friendship, Cooperation and Mutual Assistance was formed on 14 May 1955 to counter the inclusion of West Germany into NATO, which had itself been formed in 1949. It initially consisted of Albania, Bulgaria, Czechoslovakia, East Germany, Hungary, Poland, Romania and the USSR. Albania withdrew from the Pact in 1968. It was ostensibly a defensive organisation, although the tactics and strategy it developed were anything but defensive. Attack might be the best means of defence, but not at the exclusion of any form of defensive posture. The Warsaw Pact showed by its doctrine and tactics that it held considerable attack capability. It was considered a threat by all levels of both the military and political establishment, and not just those with access to considerable intelligence reports.

It has been argued that the Warsaw Pact was not capable of mounting a credible attack against the West because many of its components could not be relied upon. It is agreed that following the events in Hungary and Czechoslovakia there had to be a question mark over the reliability and loyalty of their armies. However, forces belonging to Hungary, East Germany, Poland and Bulgaria all took part in the invasion of Czechoslovakia in 1968. To assume that there was no threat from the Soviet Union, due to unreliability of its allies, was not a risk that could be taken, and was not borne out by the evidence.

The Soviet Union dominated the military alliance entirely. It used the mechanisms of the Warsaw Pact as much to keep its own satellites in order as to threaten the West. The Berlin Wall, and the fence along the whole length of the Inner German Border were designed to keep people in and western influence out. It was never designed to be a military obstacle. The goal of Soviet military strategy in Europe was a quick victory over NATO, preferably in a non-nuclear war. The aim was to defeat NATO decisively before its political and military command structure could consult and decide how to respond to an attack. Additionally it was reckoned that its allies would be more likely to remain loyal if engaged in a short and successful war against NATO.

The T62 was a Soviet Tank produced in great numbers and would have played an important part in all military operations, even though it was outmoded. It was replaced largely by the T72 (the figures indicate the year of introduction) in the Soviet Union's forces but was still the principal tank for all its allies and satellites. This one was photographed in Beirut in 1983 and had been a Syrian tank. In the front of the vehicle was a small hole where an anti-tank missile had penetrated and it had then detonated inside the vehicle, almost certainly fatally for all the occupants. (© *Museum of the Argyll and Sutherland Highlanders*)

To ensure any operation was winnable The Warsaw Pact used

every device available to it to undermine its opponents in NATO. The conflicting requirements in all countries for scarce financial resources meant that defence budgets were squeezed throughout NATO. The growth of vociferous peace movements throughout Europe, and in the USA, kept defence spending at the top of political agendas and meant that every penny spent was required to be fully justified. Such scrutiny of Western Governments and their budgets is in itself both necessary and wholly desirable, but was not an irritation which was suffered by the Warsaw Pact. These countries historically have invested a much larger share of their GDPs on military spending than was either possible or desirable in the West. Questioning of the defence establishment in the West has always been rigorous. But it is not easy to prove someone else's intention and thus Western European governments were not able to show definitively that the other side held aggressive intentions and thereby justify a demand for increased expenditure.

The TSU 23-4 was a Soviet Artillery Weapon. This vehicle was abandoned in Beirut by the Syrians in 1983. (© *Museum of the Argyll and Sutherland Highlanders*)

The Threat

The track record of the Soviet Union and its allies left the intentions of the Soviet leadership in no doubt. It maintained forces whose size was far in excess of that required for purely defensive measures. Military planners were therefore required to consider the worst-case scenario and to prepare NATO to be able to counter an attack supported by the entire Warsaw Pact. A system of government, which came into being after the Revolution, intent on eradicating all forms of imperialism, had clear expansionist aims.

We trained constantly against a number of scenarios. We were constantly tested both as individuals, and collectively. However, more senior officers at this time were rarely subjected to examination, principally because there were few mechanisms available to train regularly and to assess them. These officers were usually trained in Command Post Exercises (CPX), which would involve the exercising only of Formation Headquarters and their staffs. Also used would be Tactical Exercises Without Troops, known by the acronym of TEWT, where military tactical problems would be walked and talked through on the ground without the need to deploy 'live' soldiers. Annually there would be full-scale deployment of soldiers across the German Plain on Formation Exercises and senior officers would then be able to rehearse their drills and procedures with real soldiers. During the late 1970s and early 1980s the Brigade and Battle Group Trainer was formed. Commanders of all levels, along with their headquarters and staff could all be exercised with the aid of computers, around a large-scale tabletop map of the area selected. Once this organisation was taken into widespread use the competence of commanders and their staffs appeared to rise rapidly.

But what was the threat that we were countering? Simply, it was an invasion by a very large numbers of troops across a wide front. In straight numerical terms it was not something that we could hope to counter. On a NATO tabletop CPX involving senior chains of command which had lasted several days and included political participation right up to Downing Street, we had recorded a number of successes and had halted, at considerable cost to our own side, the invading forces. As the end of the exercise was called, the intelligence staff came into the room and emptied a bucket full of red counters, which we had been using to indicate enemy formations, all over the map. They announced that these were the second, third and fourth echelons waiting to move west across the Inner German Border. Warsaw Pact military doctrine was to achieve military superiority by surprise, speed of manoeuvre, overwhelming numbers and reinforcement of success. Where Warsaw Pact forces effected a breakthrough in NATO lines, this would be exploited and more and more troops pushed through such gaps. Those who were able to hold out would thus find themselves cut off, with a large number of enemy formations and soldiers to their rear. This was not a comforting thought.

We trained to fight a Soviet enemy, and rarely saw a Russian soldier or piece of equipment. When we did see one he never quite lived up to the chilling picture which had been painted for us. On road trips to and from Berlin, we were permitted to travel up the East German autobahn from Helmstedt, provided we did not deviate off it in any way. This was known as the Berlin Corridor. NATO did not recognise the East German authorities, and so we were not permitted to use the normal civilian frontier crossing point. A journey to Berlin was guaranteed by the Occupying Power in Germany in whose Zone one was travelling, and thus in East Germany we were under the jurisdiction of the Russians. Military traffic, even in private cars, used a special slip road to avoid the East German Immigration and Customs authorities and drove straight up to the Russian Checkpoint, passing through two metal barriers which opened and closed automatically behind. Once there, one was saluted by a Russian soldier who examined the travel papers minutely, with the smallest typing error or other discrepancy resulting immediately in a refusal of admission. This inspection usually was covertly accompanied by a request for pornography and cigarettes, whilst offering Russian military buttons and badges in return. One then had to go into the small office to have the papers further examined. Other forms of surveillance took place here, such as covertly photographing every soldier travelling. On one especially bizarre trip, I walked into this office on the day that Yuri Andropov had died in 1984. The Russian officer, fully resplendent in his uniform was watching a Black and White 1930s Hollywood musical movie with subtitles on the Russian Military TV Channel while several photographs of Andropov were draped with black ribbon.

Later, I saw and tried various Russian items of military equipment at first hand. Much of the army equipment was unreliable and of poor design. In Beirut I tried out a tracked anti-aircraft gun, and I was considerably too big for the space allocated to the crew members. Operating such a vehicle for long periods would not have been possible except by someone extremely small. The Russian protection suit against nuclear, biological and chemical (NBC) warfare was also very unpleasant to work in. It was much more rubbery than ours, and provided no outlet for sweat. It would not have been sustainable to live in, never mind fight in, for protracted periods. Although the Soviets possessed a large arsenal of biological and chemical weapons, their use is likely to have been restricted to targets far behind our front line. As Warsaw Pact soldiers could not operate for long periods in the protective clothing, the effects of any attack would be required to have dissipated before they would arrive on the scene. Additionally, the prevailing wind was from the West and would thus be blowing any chemical or biological agent into their own faces. The threat of NBC warfare was taken seriously and we undertook annual training and testing in order to prove that we could mask ourselves up in nine seconds, as well as carry out other rudimentary drills such as eating, drinking and performing the bodily functions in a hostile environment. However, equipment was scarce, and we rarely had the correct rubber gloves with which to train. The respirator was tested at least once a year in a specially designed 'gas chamber' where we burnt CS gas pellets or grenades.

It has been acknowledged that the Warsaw Pact held considerable structural flaws concerning the interaction it had with its own client states. The mighty Soviet Red Army also had its own inherent difficulties. The collective noun 'Russian' covered a number of national identities whose reliability and loyalty were questionable. The growth of Islam was identified as a problem within the Soviet army as early as the 1970s. The motivation of soldiers from some of the distant Soviet Republics to fight for a cause in Europe would not have been strong. The Soviet system of integration of these soldiers into their armed forces was exactly the opposite of our regimental system. Whereas we would deliberately keep men from one area together, such as the Argyll and Sutherland Highlanders, in order to benefit from the bond of common and shared backgrounds, the Soviets would deliberately mix men from the various Republics into different regiments. This was to try to ensure their reliability, and to prevent large-scale defections. Mixed sections of ten men, which would be commanded by a Corporal, from different Republics, would suffer racial tensions and experience language difficulties.

Soviet military doctrine, compared with our own, was somewhat ponderous. British military training encourages initiative by all ranks, and even by junior commanders. In the Warsaw Pact armies independence of command was poor, and the Marxist–Leninist system discouraged individuality. The ability of the Soviet Commander to 'seize the moment' when it occurred was extremely limited.

Since the fall of the Soviet Union, the Russian army has had some well-publicised difficulties with alcohol abuse and bullying within its ranks, resulting in many deaths. These events are thought not to be new and to have occurred before but were better hidden from public scrutiny. The interest of Soviet senior commanders in the welfare of their soldiers was not all that would have been expected in a Western European army.

Despite all this the threat was something we took extremely seriously, and we had good reason. Russian Special Forces soldiers, known as Spetznatz, used to drive or ride in commercial trucks throughout West Germany and into other parts of Europe. Their task was to become acquainted with our road networks, our ways and customs, the topography of specific areas, and generally become more familiar with Western Europe.

The threat was also something taken seriously by the Warsaw Pact soldier. He will have believed that NATO's intentions were offensive, because that is what he was told by his seniors. The Russian psyche could perhaps be summed up in the hackneyed joke – 'Just because I'm paranoid doesn't mean that they aren't out to get me!' Russia had been invaded several times, and most recently by the Germans in an act of enormous treachery. The British had also sent a small expeditionary force into Russia in 1919. The Russian memory is long, and they had good cause to be suspicious of the motives of the West. In particular, they had a fear of Germany as the most persistent and dangerous threat to the stability of Russia and the Soviet Union. They were looking at a large standing allied force based on the territory of their most feared enemy. Is it any wonder they felt insecure?

Verification Measures

To allay the fears of all sides arrangements existed for the verification of force levels and dispositions. Each of the four powers was entitled to have a military mission in the territory of the other. SOXMIS was the Soviet Military Mission to the British Forces. The object of SOXMIS, and its opposite number BRIXMIS, was officially and originally set up to 'maintain liaison between the staffs of the two Commanders in Chief.' Reciprocal arrangements for travel and circulation in each Zone of Germany existed, and each mission was to be guaranteed communications, couriers, diplomatic immunity and administrative support. In reality it was an official spying organisation. The administrative arrangements were considerably better for the Russians in SOXMIS than for the British soldiers in BRIXMIS. Russian officers would use the opportunity of being in the West to get any medical difficulty resolved in British Military Hospitals. Because Russian soldiers were accompanied by their wives, there might well be in Russia today a number of young people with British Birth Certificates issued because of their birth in a Military Hospital. The Russians also had missions in the French and American Zones, as the latter also had in the Soviet Zone.

BRIXMIS, the British equivalent contingent, was based in East Berlin. Their job too was official spying, and they used to do this by touring the country looking to assess and photograph military equipment and formations. Both sides could resort to desperate measures. On one occasion a SOXMIS vehicle was caught in a Permanently Restricted Area, on a British Training Area, digging up a latrine looking for documents and old maps. Membership of BRIXMIS could be a hazardous posting, and an Argyll Sergeant was once severely beaten up by Russian soldiers who had boxed his car in between military vehicles. This was in response to the capture of SOXMIS staff who had been found in an area of Permanent Restriction. Their car too had been boxed in and held for some hours until the arrival of the Military Police to escort them back to their compound. But SOXMIS were not the only ones to sneak into Restricted Areas. Both sides would get away with as much as they could, and it became a kind of game. When not involved in such activities the members of the teams would socialise from time to time. A Russian speaking Argyll officer, who was a BRIXMIS operator, owes many hangovers to Russian hospitality, and now has friends in many parts of the Russian establishment.

Other verification measures existed. It was a requirement of both sides to inform the others of all troop movements over a certain size. Exercises and training could not take place within about 25 kilometres of the East German Border. British troops frequently enjoyed the skiing in the Harz Mountains. This and other such adventure-training activities had to be undertaken in civilian clothing and with demilitarised vehicles.

British Military Dispositions

The British Forces based in Germany were all under the umbrella of NATO. There was a considerable air force presence with every type of aircraft capability. The British Forces were split in two. The 1st British Corps, whose Headquarters were at Bielefeld, commanded the forward element. Under this were four British Divisions. During the early 1980s the 2nd Division was returned to the UK and based in York, but with a reinforcement role. This was undertaken primarily on cost grounds, and it thus had a much-reduced tactical and strategic value as a result. The total manpower in the Corps at any one time would be about 50,000 troops. Further west in Germany was the Rear Combat Zone, reaching into Holland and Belgium. This was to maintain lines of communications through the Low Countries, and employed about another 10,000 soldiers. In addition, in Rheindahlen, was the Headquarters of the Northern Army Group (NORTHAG), which commanded the British Corps, a Dutch Division, a Belgian Division Corps, a German Corps and latterly some smaller American formations as well. The Commander of this organisation was always a senior British General.

The area in which British garrisons were located was, in most cases, ground for which we were responsible in the event of conflict. However, a NORTHAG out-loading plan could be full of hazards and difficulties. Troops going to their immediate areas of responsibility might have to cross the routes of others, similarly out-loading, going to their own allocated areas. These plans were exercised frequently, and as fully as possible, but never was the actual plan tried out for fear that it would reveal our intended dispositions to the Warsaw Pact. Exercises would be carried out over ground which we would require to defend in war but a variety of scenarios would be tried, and again our intended positions in the event of war were kept secret. As a platoon commander it was not deemed necessary for me to know what ground I had been allocated to defend. However, as a Company Commander, I reconnoitred my area of responsibility on a number of occasions and made detailed written plans of my intended dispositions in a notebook which was kept under very strict security when not being used.

For two years I was a staff officer in the Headquarters of the 1st Armoured Division. This was based in Verden, situated about half way between Hanover and Bremerhaven. My day-to-day job involved responsibility for all forms of training which included exercise planning, allocation of training ammunition and ranges, and the assessment of standards to which I had objected when younger. In war, when training and simulation would cease, I became a part of the operations staff, and was responsible for commanding the Divisional Commander's Forward Tactical Headquarters, consisting of three tracked armoured vehicles. This was the best job in the Division. It required me to go almost everywhere in the Divisional area and at the same time to be away from the tedious scrutiny of my senior officers. The Divisional Commander, a Major General and his small team, consisting of the Artillery and Engineer commanders, used us frequently as a small hard headquarters from which to command events and to travel to visit other headquarters or units. I was therefore required to know all that was going on and to keep abreast of the situation. It was a key position. In war this job would also have been one of the more survivable ones. The principal Divisional Headquarters, which commanded approximately 15,000 men, operated with two identical groups of vehicles. Each group consisted of twelve armoured personnel carriers laid out in a cruciform shape. At any one time one of the groups would be the operating and active headquarters, known as 'Main'. The other group of vehicles would be stripping down, moving or setting up and would be known as 'Step Up'. Command in 'Main' would last about twelve hours before switching to 'Step Up' which would then become 'Main'. Staff would move between the two in carefully coordinated stages. It is possible to conceal such headquarters in towns, buildings or woods. However, large organisations such as this, accompanied by the entourage required for its administration, would leave huge thermal and electronic signatures, as well as tracks and other physical signs of movement. A Divisional Headquarters would be liable to early discovery and would be a most attractive target for aircraft or artillery, perhaps delivering chemical or biological weapons. I was always very happy to escape such a monolith with my small team of vehicles.

All units and headquarters were liable to be called out, at any time of the day or night, either in an emergency or to have their readiness assessed. This liability became greater the further down the command chain one was. As an infantry battalion one could be called out by every level of superior headquarters. The exercise would start on receipt of a telephoned code word which would trigger a pre-prepared plan to get the maximum number of men, vehicles and equipment out of the gate within a specific and short time-scale. It could give rise to some amusing situations. On one occasion a colleague of mine, quite legitimately coming into camp at about 6.45 one morning after a night on the town, found his complete platoon and vehicles driving out the gate past him. He took a long time to live that down.

Military Problems

Professionally, being based in Germany was a challenge. The skills and tactics required for the infantry to operate from armoured vehicles are different to those for other more conventional forms of soldiering. Time is needed to train and master these skills. The training would follow a set annual pattern, allowing a progressive build-up in order to be able to operate in large formations. We would start with individual skills, such as fitness, shooting, and living in the field on what we could carry on our backs. We would then progress to operating in our Armoured Personnel Carriers and eventually we would all operate together, working with other units and formation. This was not the simple task it sounds. For example, infantry in their vehicles could not operate at the same speed as tanks, and considerable practice was required to ensure that we could work effectively together. The space to exercise in large formations, in an 'all arms' environment, does not exist in Europe. Every year seven units would go to the Prairies in Canada where there is room on a Canadian training area for the infantry, tanks and artillery to all operate together whilst firing live ammunition.

There were two obstacles to mastering these skills. The first of these was the requirement to take our place in the *roulement* in Northern Ireland. The regiment completed tours in 1972, 1976, 1978 and 1979. A tour length was initially four months but was later raised to six. Training for a tour took a further twelve weeks. At the end of the tour we would take up to four weeks leave, thus considerably reducing the time available to master the necessary skills and achieve the required standards to a maximum of four months. The pressure on soldiers during these times was considerable, and in a survey we discovered that one particular group of our soldiers had slept in their own beds for only seventy-two nights in a calendar year. The effects on soldiers' families were considerable.

The other pressure, far more insidious, was the shortage of defence funding. As a result of the political pressures on the defence budget we were frequently undergoing swingeing cuts to fuel, training ammunition and vehicle spare parts. This meant that the training we undertook was often half-hearted, unrealistic, and large exercises could be cut short because funding was reduced. The 1970s was a turbulent period for the armed forces, with questioning as to whether we were necessary, and if so, in what form and size. There was a considerable rise in the number, strength and noise of peace and anti-nuclear movements. Society had forgotten the realities of war, and most people could not comprehend the requirement for an expensive standing army based in Germany. The political and financial classes could not decide whether we were an expensive necessity or a luxury. We were an irritant and an easy target when money was required elsewhere in the national budget. We felt, and I think were, unloved!

This was reflected in a number of areas. Purchase and renewal of capital equipment was almost nonexistent. Our armoured personnel carriers were outdated and could be unreliable. Our rates of pay did not keep pace with inflation, and my annual pay rise in 1978 resulted in my being 50 pence a month worse off after the pay rise than before it once the additional charges for food and accommodation were levied. Morale was therefore low, and, to an extent this became reflected in the discipline and behaviour of some parts of the army. The effects of tours in Northern Ireland, the poor state of our equipment and our conditions of service meant that we were probably incapable of carrying out our task. This was an unsatisfactory period for the regiment. It is important for soldiers involved in difficult and sometimes dangerous tasks to feel that their contribution is important and valued. The words of Rudyard Kipling, written many years earlier, were relevant to the seventies and eighties.

Oh it's Tommy this, an' Tommy that, an' 'Tommy go away';
But it's 'Thank you Mister Atkins' when the band begins to play.
…

It's Tommy this an' Tommy that, an' 'Chuck him out the brute!'
But it's 'Saviour of 'is country' when the guns begin to shoot.
…

Then it's Tommy this an' Tommy that, an' 'Tommy 'ow's yer soul?'
But it's 'Thin Red Line of 'eroes' when the drums begin to roll.

The requirement for cheaper armed forces also resulted in some ill-advised changes on a more strategic level. The move back to the UK of the 2nd Division has already been mentioned. In addition the Brigade level formation was disposed of because it was believed that the Divisional level could command and direct right down to units. This was like removing the entire middle management out of an organisation of 1,450,000 people. It was a simple cost-cutting measure, although it was accompanied by considerable reassurance from politicians and senior military officers that the same effectiveness could be delivered by fewer troops. Also cut considerably was what in military parlance is known as the tail – primarily logistical units, holdings and capability. The knock-on effect of these cuts resulted in the Americans moving two Brigades into Northern Germany (their area of responsibility was usually considerably further south), and the American political establishment starting to ask why they were doing what Europeans should be doing for themselves.

An attack by the Warsaw Pact in the 1970s and early 1980s would have found the Allies in Europe ill prepared. It is likely that the Warsaw Pact armies could have reached the Rhine within a few days, even from a standing start, provided nuclear weapons were not used.

Lacking the necessary population and finance, the UK is not able to provide a large standing army. For some time now our strategy has been to have a small, well-trained and equipped, manoeuvrable army. The army in Germany in the 1970s did not reflect this approach. This was potentially extremely serious and the effect of such inbuilt weakness, had it become apparent in any Warsaw Pact assault, would have been to reduce the nuclear threshold. Subsequent Conservative and Labour Governments, by allowing the army in North West Europe to fall into a relative state of disrepair, had made the likelihood of nuclear war greater.

Allied Forces

As has already been stated, military command in Northern Germany lay with the commander of NORTHAG. This consisted of formations provided by the Belgians, the Dutch, the Germans and our own 1st British Corps. All of these organisations came with their own unique difficulties.

The Dutch Corps was very heavily reliant on reservists who had only ever received conscript training. The Dutch Government was reluctant to maintain any sizeable presence, and so the majority of the soldiers and their equipment was in Holland, over 150 miles to the West of their allocated positions. There was very little chance that they would be in place in the event of a surprise attack or a short warning scenario. We frequently carried out training on the same areas as their soldiers. We found them fascinating. Haircuts were optional and so in the trendy 1970s many of their male soldiers had hair down their backs and wore hairnets. Drugs were a problem in the Dutch Army long before it became a factor in ours. The Dutch military had a trade union to act for them, which prescribed certain military practices such as training over a weekend. It was interesting to see that when the introduction of a trade union in the British Army became a discussion topic it didn't carry much support from our soldiers. They could see that if it developed the way of the Dutch model it would be counter to military professionalism.

The Belgian Corps was similar to the Dutch in that most of it was in Belgium. One attraction of the Belgians was that they took their cuisine seriously, and they possessed an officers' club near Soest, beside the Mohnesee Dam of Dambusters fame. This club employed fully trained and qualified high-grade chefs reluctantly undergoing their National

Service, and the food was both the most exquisite and the cheapest in the whole of Germany. They were very different to our 'slop jockeys'!

The German Corps was a very different matter. Although largely made up of conscripts, they were much better trained. The psyche of the German soldier was also, understandably, completely different. He was defending his homeland which was under threat. At senior levels there was concern that the Germans might not obey the orders of their British commander. NATO doctrine was to be prepared to give ground in order to buy time for the politicians to sort out their response to the aggression. This trade-off did not sit easily with the German military, who could be surrendering their own home areas. And they only too well remembered the behaviour of the Russian soldiers towards German civilians in 1945. Therefore, it was feared that the German Corps might defy NATO orders and take ground by moving into East Germany as far and as fast as possible and before any ceasefire could be arranged.

The Nuclear Option

General Sir John Hackett in his book *The Third World War* describes the build-up of an imaginary war, which results in nuclear strikes on Birmingham and Minsk. Horrific as it reads it does show that a nuclear exchange would be survivable and it would not preface the disintegration of a nation. There are few facts and much scare mongering about the effects, social and otherwise of a nuclear strike. The greatest danger resulting from the detonation of a nuclear weapon is not the immediate after-effects of such a strike, catastrophic as that would be over a large area, but the realisation that the use of such weapons is manageable. This could result in a consequent escalation and frequency of their devastating use.

In the event of a Warsaw Pact invasion it is unlikely that NATO would have been able to resist the numerical superiority for long. NATO's qualitative edge would not have lasted and the use of nuclear weapons would then have been inevitable. It was the threat of such use which prevented the Warsaw Pact from moving westwards. Relatively widespread use of small-scale atomic munitions (ADM) would have been likely from an early stage in a conflict. The only practical way of destroying a submarine is by an ADM. Use of such munitions in the air early on would also have been likely. To stop the advance of Warsaw Pact armoured formations on land it would have been necessary to use ADMs to destroy the larger solid autobahn and rail bridges. Such uses would then have started a nuclear escalation and who knows where it would have ended? The procedures for requesting and granting nuclear release were frequently exercised by all levels, including senior political figures, during Command Post Exercises. These also provided the opportunity to practise and work through the events and actions which would be required subsequently in the event of nuclear release being granted. The participation of Downing Street in our CPXs occurred so that all levels of command and control could practise the requesting and granting of nuclear release. It was believed that, typically, Margaret Thatcher would insist on taking part in these exercises herself, and make her staff go through the complete briefing procedures when such a request had been made.

The German view of nuclear release was understandably different from ours or the other allies. It was the devastation of German territory and the deaths of German civilians which was being discussed and decided. There was, reputedly, once a discussion between Margaret Thatcher and Chancellor Kohl and their staffs about the requirement and mechanism to authorise nuclear release. The British view was that the NATO military authorities would need to make such a request after about twenty-four hours. Such authority would take about twenty-four hours to obtain, and actual release would be required in the period between forty-eight and seventy-two hours after an invasion. It has been claimed that Chancellor Kohl said that he would never give his authority in any such meeting. The story goes that Margaret Thatcher came back with the withering reply:

'But Chancellor, you would not be invited to the discussion.'

The nuclear age, whether we like it or not, is here to stay. Nuclear weapons, having been invented, are not going to disappear. The part played by nuclear weapons in maintaining peace in Europe since the end of the Second World War is unequivocal. Their presence was a deterrent to aggression. Even the new Archbishop of Canterbury, Dr Rowan Williams, acknowledged the part played by possession of such weapons when in his recent Reith Lecture he said:

> Intercontinental Missile Technology designed to carry out mass destruction makes nonsense of traditional ideas of defending your territory; you have to rely on strategic means, above all deterrent counter threats when things look menacing.

The Cold War was a time of menace and danger. Events surrounding the Berlin Blockade and Airlift, the building of The Berlin Wall and the Cuban Missile Crisis demonstrated this only too well. We know now that the Soviet Union's economy was starting to stagnate in the 1970s and 1980s, and this would eventually result in its demise in the early 1990s. It is therefore feasible today to say that the threat offered by the Soviet Union and its satellites might not have been as great as was feared at the time. But the perception of what President Reagan described as the 'Evil Empire' was that there was a real threat to European societies and political institutions. In such matters perception is everything. Subsequent revelations of reality are of academic interest only. If anyone doubts the strong perception that very real dangers and threats were faced, they should travel to areas close to what was the Inner German Border and ask any German citizen.

Lifestyle

There were, and still are, a number of anachronisms about living in Germany. As a member of the Forces one is entitled to purchase cheap petrol at some civilian filling stations by presenting coupons purchased at a discount from the unit. Normally BP has the contract, but it can vary from year to year. In the NAAFI Service shops a ration card is still needed to buy cheap tea and coffee, as well as duty free tobacco and alcohol. The ration on all these items is so large that it is difficult to exceed one's allowance, and the main purpose of the card is to ensure that such goods are purchased only by those entitled to them.

Generally, units are based in garrison towns, and Osnabruck and Minden (the most recent German garrisons for the regiment) are classic examples. A number of units would be based in barracks around the town. The barracks were frequently old German military establishments, and would contain furniture stamped with swastikas, and other signs of their wartime occupation and use. Garrisons would have all the typical hallmarks of such towns, familiar down the centuries. Local bars and clubs would cater principally for the soldier, attracting the inevitable following of local girls and sometimes upset men! Such establishments could become the centre of trouble from time to time, and the customary Saturday exchanges between soldiers and the locals, or even just between soldiers, were frequent. Sadly, in Osnabruck, where we were based near to two other Scottish Regiments, the Queen's Own Highlanders and the Royal Scots Dragoon Guards, relations between these groups of Scottish soldiers were not good. Surprisingly we got on better at all levels with the Inniskilling Dragoon Guards, an Irish regiment.

But life was not generally lived in a British ghetto. Great efforts were made to maintain good relations with the local German inhabitants and the authorities. Emphasis was placed on soldiers learning German, and language courses were readily available and a requirement for some. As an inducement, a one-off payment was made to any soldier reaching a specific level of achievement in the language and he or she would wear a badge showing this skill. Many soldiers became fluent in German, usually through the good influences of their girlfriends and families. A number of soldiers would choose to socialise only on the German 'net'. Some fifty of them married local girls in Osnabruck, and about half that number in Minden, most of whom chose to remain in Germany.

However, it was possible to live life almost entirely as one would live it in Britain. In all garrisons there would be British run shops offering everything British, from insurance policies to Sunblest bread. When we moved into Minden the NAAFI stocked Irn Bru and scotch pies especially for us. Travel agencies offering cut-price trips back home abounded. Medical clinics were staffed by British civilian doctors, while the Service Schools, following the English curriculum, employed teachers specially recruited in Britain. The British Forces Broadcasting Service was the starting point for the careers of many show business personalities and since the late 1980s there has also been a Forces TV Service offering programmes from both the BBC and ITV.

Alastair Campbell and two Russian Officers in Winhhoek, Namibia, in 1995. *(© Museum of the Argyll and Sutherland Highlanders)*

For recreation, British garrisons provided much in the way of sporting facilities for soldiers and their families. Cars could be purchased duty free, and we ran our own registration system with distinctive and readily identified number plates. These changed in the 1980s because the IRA started targeting soldiers through their British Forces number plates. We were encouraged to buy left-hand drive cars and to obtain German registrations. Those with right-hand drive cars reverted to normal British plates.

Conclusion

The Cold War, to a soldier, was a real conflict, and one that had a profound effect on the lives of its combatants. Soldiers of the Argyll and Sutherland Highlanders were required to observe disciplines which normally applied in times of tension or wartime. These sometimes surreal experiences could not be imagined by people at home, unaware that such depths of hidden conflict existed in the 20th century and in times of apparent peace. They were, however, an excellent training ground for other theatres. Experience of tours in Germany taught how to conduct fast, fluid, mobile armoured operations. Although the results of these many years of training did not become evident until the Gulf War of 1990-91 and the more recent conflict in Iraq, the success of these operations was due to military grounding across the plains of Northern Germany. The many skills, the discipline and the patience required of a soldier today, as well as much of the operational experience and reputation of the Regiment, are derived from the grounding of the tours in Germany.

The opportunities offered by being able to live overseas were memorable and somewhat unique. A military force based in a foreign country, by invitation rather than by force, is uncommon. It was also strange to feel safer and more welcome on the streets of German towns and cities than on the streets of the United Kingdom, especially in Northern Ireland.

Life abroad for soldiers offers men a shared and common experience which provides a 'glue' or a bond for many years. The Regimental Association, the welfare and social arm of the Regiment, principally but not exclusively for ex-soldiers or veterans, is, as a result, a tightly knit organisation.

Life in Germany, where we could all see the threat in the form of SOXMIS vehicles, as well as the existence of a very real and forbidding

Inner German Border, gave us a military *raison d'être*. We knew that the enemy existed, and that he posed a threat to us. The visible and verifiable Cold War tensions were easy to contend with. Today, when the threats are more insidious and hidden, it is an irony that we are not the only ones who are perhaps wondering whether the Cold War could have been 'The Good Old Days'.

Bibliography

W. LaFeber, *America, Russia, and the Cold War, 1945-1992*, (London: McGraw-Hill, c1993).

R. Crockatt, *The fifty years war: the United States and the Soviet Union in world politics, 1941–1991*, (London: Routledge, 1995).

Arne Westad (Ed) *Reviewing the Cold War: approaches, interpretations, and theory*, (London: Frank Cass, 2000).

J. L. Gaddis, *We now know: rethinking Cold War history*, (Oxford: Clarendon Press, c1998, 1997).

D. Wilson, *The sum of things*, (Staplehurst: Spellmount, 2001).

General Sir J. Hackett, *The Third World War. A Future History*, (London: Sphere Books), 1978.

Above: HMS *Dreadnought* arriving at Rosyth for routine docking in December 1963.
Below: Home fleet at Rosyth: HMS *Kenya,* May 1958.

Chapter 6

WILL THEY BLOW US A' TAE HELL?

STRATEGIES AND OBSTACLES FOR THE DISARMAMENT MOVEMENT IN SCOTLAND

Brian P. Jamison

The UK's Vanguard class Trident SSBN and SLBM, stationed at submarine base Faslane and serviced at Royal Navy Armaments Depot (RNAD) Coulport, inspired both the British and international disarmament movements to make clear their intentions to have the Trident system decommissioned and promptly towed from the river Clyde in the west of Scotland. While Scottish civil society learned to accept the presence of both the US and UK Polaris systems in its lochs after the early 1960s, protest groups like the Campaign for Nuclear Disarmament (CND), its Scottish equivalent (SCND) and Trident Ploughshares attempted to convince the general public that Trident was the unacceptable proliferation of such weapons and utilised an assortment of strategies to make this point clear.[1]

---

[1] During a discussion with Iain Leitch, former Labour councillor for Dumbarton District Council, it was argued that lawful ownership of nuclear weapons was partially based on racially motivated guidelines. While nuclear-weapon states like the US, UK and Israel were free to possess such weapons free of harassment; India, North Korea and Pakistan were chastised for such development and consistently reminded of their futility. Furthermore, following Gulf War II activists argued that while UN inspectors could not find Iraqi weapons of mass destruction they could easily locate such items in the west of Scotland. Interview with Iain Leitch, former Labour Councillor for Dumbarton District Council, (07/03/03)

Therefore, when interpreting the history of the disarmament movement's experience with the UK deterrent several issues need to be addressed: the composition of the movement from 1979–1999 and how the anti-Polaris movement compared with the disarmament movement's Trident campaign; the strategies employed by the anti-Trident movement in its opposition to the Polaris replacement; the obstacles it encountered and the accomplishment of the disarmament movement after the Vanguard class began round-the-clock patrols in the North Atlantic. While a number of issues still remain, it is first necessary to retrace the events that led to the creation of the British disarmament movement.

The Anti-Polaris Movement

Without the creation of the political pressure group, British CND, both the Scottish and worldwide debate about such weaponry would have been far less developed by the time the Thatcher government opted to acquire the US Trident system in July 1980. Thirteen years prior to the formation of Greenpeace and four decades before the first series of non-violent direct-actions by Trident Ploughshares, articles written by Bertrand Russell and J. B. Priestley questioning the validity of nuclear weapons inspired concerned citizens to establish CND in London in 1958. According to the former Labour Party leader Michael Foot, the creation of CND 'made our country [Britain] the most active and vocal in the world in attempting to rouse mankind to an awareness of the nuclear horror.'[2] Consequently, the London-based organisation provided the spark that inspired the creation of the Scottish campaign that same year. The autonomous SCND was formed in Glasgow with its own unique objections initially focused on the testing of nuclear weapons and the increasing threat of nuclear warfare. The group was not a pacifist organisation in the sense that it was not committed to opposing the possession of all weapons, but it was concerns with local issues that

---

[2] M. Foot, *Dr. Strangelove, I Presume*, (London: Victor Gollancz, 1999), p. 68, 69, 72.

ultimately characterised the distinctly Scottish aspect of SCND.[3] With the installation of the US Navy's Polaris fleet in the Holy Loch after 1961, the SCND's initial concerns were considerably displaced and became directly focused on nuclear-powered ballistic missile submarines. Robust support from the likes of the British Communist and Scottish Labour Parties, Scotland's local authorities, trade unions and thousands of ordinary citizens throughout Britain fuelled this movement at its earliest stages.

It was the physical presence of the US Polaris force that initially bolstered the SCND's determination to have the sea-based deterrent removed from Scottish lochs. After CND marches to Aldermaston in April 1958, Conservative Prime Minister Harold MacMillan convinced Washington to sell the UK Skybolt in exchange for the US Navy's use of the Holy Loch as a forward-operating submarine base for its own Polaris fleet in March 1960. It was this decision that thrust Scotland into the 'centre of superpower and military block rivalries' as the arrival of Fleet Ballistic Missile Refit Site One, USS *Proteus*, and the first American Polaris boats incited an intense response both north of the Border and throughout the wider UK.[4] Despite the then maturing state of the Anglo-American special relationship a foreign nuclear presence in Scotland provoked inactive supporters of the disarmament movement to respond as marches soon attracted considerable attention throughout the British press. On 4 March 1961 the SCND, working in conjunction with the highly energetic Direct Action Committee Against Nuclear Weapons (DAC), gathered roughly 1,000 participants and marched from Dunoon to the Holy Loch in opposition to its American defender. That year, supporting demonstrations were also held on 14 May, and on 20–21 May, with the latter representing an escalation of the movement's efforts.[5]

---

[3] A. Carter, *Campaigns for Peace: British peace movements in the 20th Century since 1945*, (Manchester: MUP, 1992), p. 153.

[4] M. Spaven, *Fortress Scotland: A Guide to the Military Presence*, (London: Pluto Press, 1983), p. 1.

[5] The 14 May march attracted roughly 2,000. While the 20 May demonstration executed a 'sea action' by attempting to board US boats, the 21 May protest featured a 'land action' to occupy two piers used by submarine crews. R. K. S. Taylor and C. Pritchard, *The protest makers: the*

However, in the midst of a Cold War the deterrence value of the Polaris system, regardless of its foreign status, soothed much of Britain's post-1945 security concerns and thus remained firmly in place. Nevertheless, these four demonstrations established a precedent and served as a useful model for future demonstrations in both Scotland and the international community.

It has to be kept in mind that the system was received in Scotland with a lingering degree of ambivalence that was later duplicated with the arrival of the Royal Navy's Vanguard class. With the bombing of Hiroshima and Nagasaki a not-so-distant memory, Scottish reactions to the US Polaris presence generally proved predictable if not monumental. After the explosions over Japan worldwide hysteria with nuclear weaponry was reinforced by Cold War anxieties: fears which were dictated by the state of relations between the US and USSR. Author Robert H. Patterson went as far as stating that the UK's 'reduced status in the international community' post-1945 had 'manifested itself in a fear of nuclear war.'[6] Therefore, the introduction of the stealthy rocket-firing nuclear submarine to the Holy Loch highlighted technological improvements in the field of nuclear deterrence and ultimately served as a cause for great concern throughout the UK.[7] Polaris in Scotland ultimately turned fear of nuclear war into a rallying force with the song *Ding Dong Dollar* becoming the anthem of the Scottish anti-Polaris movement (Page..?).[8] Though unclear, the following deployment of the UK's own Polaris system to the Gare Loch in 1968 may also have played a significant role in the historic victory of nationalist Winifred

---

British nuclear disarmament movement of 1958-1965, twenty years on, (London: Permagon Press, 1980), p. 138.

[6] R. H. Patterson, *Britain's Strategic Nuclear Deterrent: From Before the V-Bomber to Beyond Trident*, (London: Frank Cass & Co. Ltd., 1997), p. 123.

[7] The stealth of the SSBN was considered more desirable than the medium-range airborne deterrent.

[8] *Ding Dong Dollar* was written when Glaswegian John Mack heard George MacLeod of the Iona Community say 'You cannot spend a dollar when you are dead'. John Smith got the basic chorus idea, then it was refined and Jim McLean joined in the working up of the verses. Interview with John Powles, Glasgow Caledonian University Centre for Political Song, (08/03/03)

Ewing in the 1967 Hamilton by-election, allowing the Scottish National Party (SNP) to mobilise the sense that Scotland might at some point be better off as an independent state. However, the US Navy did have its share of Scottish supporters. A former US serviceman stationed at the Holy Loch in 1961 described the reception of USS *Porteus* as 'cordial' and the Provost, Ms C. S. McPhail, expressed her hope that the Americans would be treated, not as visitors, but as part of the fabric of the town.'[9] While the US presence was indeed the centre of controversy in 1961 Scotland, economic considerations often countered unilateralist arguments as American sailors on shore leave brought their hard-earned dollars to surrounding communities. Nevertheless, by the early 1970s this conflict of interests subsided considerably as Scots dismissed the company of American and British systems and became more concerned with issues pertaining to everyday living. If the disarmament movement hoped to inspire the decommissioning of the UK's own Trident deterrent after 1980 it would therefore need to overcome a history of security and safe operation, and seriously consider the potential for substantial unemployment in Scotland. For the disarmament movement to reach its objective a suitable response to the benefits of Trident had first to be effectively delivered.

The Anti-Trident Movement

The Thatcher government's decision to procure and operate Trident from the Clyde at the height of the Cold War encouraged the SCND to establish numerous connections and explore new strategies, achieving a superior degree of complexity to that of the Polaris campaign.[10] Though the self-governing SCND often spearheaded anti-Trident activities in Scotland throughout this period, it also frequently utilised a two-tier system of interdependency that allowed the organisation to network with the international disarmament movement, recognise and support local

---

[9] *SubRon 14 and Scotland*, Available: http://thistlegroup.net/holyloch/history.htm, (13/03.03).
[10] Trident was able to deliver a maximum of 128 warheads per boat with each at least eight times more powerful than the bomb dropped on Hiroshima.

groups throughout Scotland and work in unison with specialist sections that either disrupted the operation of Trident, applied considerable political pressure, or challenged the intrinsic worth of nuclear weaponry. Furthermore, this loosely knit pattern of co-operation allowed the movement to monitor rigorously Trident-related activities while the SCND often acted as a collection point for intelligence. Information for the SCND was then dispersed amongst other independent organisations as well as local groups and specialist sections and used either to disrupt the operation of the system through planned actions or eventually to assist in organised demonstrations. Therefore, the circulation of information between individual bodies served to strengthen the disarmament movement's efforts in Scotland as a whole.

While SCND's efforts were consistently reinforced by CND, over the years it maintained cooperation with other independent organisations such as Greenpeace UK, the Scottish Campaign to Resist the Atomic Menace (SCRAM), the Nuclear Free Local Authorities (NFLA) and Trident Ploughshares while also creating the alternative Scottish Campaign Against Trident (SCAT).[11] Both Greenpeace UK and SCRAM viewed nuclear weapons as an environmental issue, yet from 1987 the former demonstrated around the world against nuclear-armed and nuclear-powered warships while SCRAM temporarily addressed the Trident issue in Scotland as the SCND's popularity peaked during the early 1980s.[12] These groups therefore served more of a supportive role to the disarmament movement. The NFLA, Ploughshares and SCAT were considerably more aggressive in their approach to the UK deterrent. Both the CND and the NFLA attempted to publicise the effects of nuclear war and the false sense of security that Civil Defence plans provided.[13] In

---

[11] For examples of groups within the international movement and their work in Scotland see Angie Zelter, *Trident on Trial: The Case for People's Disarmament*, (Edinburgh: Luath Press, 2001).

[12] Formed in November 1975 as an umbrella group of Friends of the Earth, the Conservation Society and the Edinburgh University Ecological Society, SCRAM ended when it merged with Friends of the Earth in the early 1990s. Interview with Peter Roche, co-founder of SCRAM, (27/03/03).

[13] P. Byrne, *The Campaign for Nuclear Disarmament*, (London: Routledge, 1988), p. 167.

addition, like the DAC of the 1960s, Ploughshares believed there was a distinct need for non-violent direct action and did not operate from Scotland exclusively because Trident-related sites were scattered throughout Britain, with each considered by the organisation to be legitimate targets for actions.[14] However, SCAT was simply an attempt by the SCND to widen its own appeal. Though dates are unclear, it was formed when the SCND considered that a broader-based campaign against Trident was necessary to take account of the extent of opposition to the system even amongst supporters of the nuclear deterrent. SCAT was a successful campaign in that it reached and was supported by a wide spectrum of Scottish society, though the campaign was merged with SCND when Trident was initially deployed in the early 1990s.[15] Nevertheless, the creation of a vast network allowed the movement in Scotland to establish credible links with both domestic and foreign disarmament groups, making the Government's objectives all the more difficult.

Local groups were the primary unit of organisation for SCND while highly-active independent specialist sections often functioned as the disarmament movement's eyes and ears. Though it was the responsibility of SCND both to promote and facilitate their activities, over a twenty-year period, an undetermined number of local groups was established from Aberdeen to Dumbarton and Dunfermline. Unfortunately, the permanence of these groups varied as their numbers experienced a steady decline after the early 1980s, and further deterioration following the collapse of the Soviet Union, presenting figures that often fluctuated according to international and/or local developments. The key function of the specialist section was to further the cause of the disarmament movement as sections like Christian, Student and Trade Union CND spread the message of unilateral

---

[14] Based in Norfolk, it was launched in Hiroshima, Gothenburg, Gent, Edinburgh and London in May 1998. Interview with David McKenzie, media officer for Trident Ploughshares, (12/03/03).

[15] SCAT was chaired by Iain Leitch of Dumbarton District Council. Interview with Ian Leitch, (07/03/03).

disarmament throughout Scotland's religious communities, universities and unions.[16] Faslane Peace Camp, Nukewatch UK and Rosyth Watch were indispensable specialist sections, diligent in monitoring and blocking the transport of Polaris and Trident warheads to and from the Coulport/Faslane area, observing and sometimes attempting to obstruct submarine patrols entering and exiting the Clyde or surveying refitting and refuelling operations of nuclear-powered submarines at Rosyth Royal Dockyard.[17] Of these, Faslane Peace Camp had established itself as the most recognisable specialist section in Scotland, if not in all of Britain. Inspired by Greenham Common Woman's Camp, in June 1982 members of the SCND, the anti-nuclear group Parents for Survival and the Ecology Party established Faslane Peace Camp with the assistance of Strathclyde Regional Council. Furthermore, the SCND also concentrated on applying political pressure to Trident together with specialist sections like Green, Labour, Liberal and SNP CND, which encouraged their respective MPs to campaign against the proliferation of nuclear weapons.[18] However, Paul Byrne, Senior Lecturer in Politics at Loughborough University, acknowledged that certain sections had been accused of being more 'concerned with importing political disagreements into the movement rather than exporting the unilateralist message' from time to time.[19]

In exploring the history of the disarmament movement during this period, general statistics pertaining to the body of the anti-Trident movement in Scotland as a whole are unclear and records pertaining to the SCND's local groups, specialist sections, executive committees and chairpersons were quite vague. Scouring the SCND's Annual General

---

[16] Christian CND was composed of many denominations, questioning the morality of Trident. Origins and related statistics were unavailable.

[17] Inspired by Nukewatch US, peace activists concerned with the 'elimination' of Polaris and Trident organised Polaris Watch in the summer of 1985, which later became Nukewatch UK. It conducted a program to monitor and expose the transportation of nuclear weapons in unmarked trucks. Interview with Jane Tallents of Nukewatch UK, (006/03/03). Information on Rosyth Watch was unavailable. Interview with J. Ainslie, head administrator of SCND, (25/03/03).

[18] Interview with Dr Jim Taggart, Labour CND, (28/02/03).

[19] Byrne, *The Campaign for Nuclear Disarmament*, p. 123.

Meeting notes has revealed that executive committees and selected chairpersons were established during the early 1980s and came together on a yearly basis to discuss campaign priorities. Records pertaining to membership were just slightly more informative. According to Byrne, British CND offered two types of membership; national members who paid an annual subscription to national CND and local members who subscribed to their local group. He further acknowledged that the CND's total membership at the end of 1986 was roughly 86,000, based largely in England rather than the rest of the UK, and by 1988 eighty-nine per cent of CND members lived in England, six per cent in Scotland, five per cent in Wales and less than one per cent in Ireland.[20] To both the CND and Scottish campaign's disadvantage, these figures alone represented a distinct minority of overall population percentages. Finally, Burn described the social composition of CND's membership in the 1980s as comparable to that of the 1960s with membership remaining predominantly middles class, 'overwhelmingly' potential Labour voters, evenly balanced between the sexes and concentrated in the 25–40 age-group.[21] However, a rigid portrayal such as this was inevitably subject to numerous exceptions.

Strategies of the anti-Trident movement

In March 1986 Margaret Morton, in the left-nationalist magazine *Radical Scotland,* explained that, 'it was essential to build up opposition to Trident in the early stages, before it gained political credibility and

---

[20] Similar to local groups, membership statistics for disarmament groups remained blurred due to enlistment inconsistencies that were often determined by international and local events or those who wished to retain their anonymity. When HMS Vanguard arrived to Faslane in October 1992 SCND gathered 100 new memberships, though many never renewed. Anonymity was an issue best exemplified by members of the Faslane Peace Camp who often referred to themselves on a first name basis only. Interview with J. Ainslie, head administrator of SCND, (25/03/03) Peter Roche, SCRAM, (27/03/03) and Iain Leitch, former Labour Councillor for Dumbarton District Council, (07/03/03) . Byrne, *Campaign for Nuclear Disarmament*, p. 55.

[21] One-third of CND's members also belonged to a trade union, one-quarter to a political party, one fifth to a church and two-thirds of CND also members of other peace organizations.

before investment decisions were made.'[22] In its drive to discourage Trident's construction and eventual operation from Scotland the disarmament movement conducted numerous campaigns which included Greenpeace UK's 1987 'Nuclear Free Seas' strategy, the CND's early 1990s' 'Scrap Trident' campaign and Ploughshares 1998 'Tri-denting It' action. The CND's 1985 'Basic Case' strategy proved most controversial. In the aftermath of the 1983 General Election the Thatcher government's consideration of both Cruise and Trident encouraged the CND to integrate their policies against these specific systems and focus public opinion more on the basic fundamentals of nuclear disarmament. However, it was argued that progress with the Trident campaign at a national level 'writhed' because the strategy detracted considerably from a well-understood purpose, opposition to two distinct systems, with a concept 'so vague as to make it meaningless'.[23] Helen Steven, activist, author and member of the Iona Community, further agreed that CND's emphasis on Cruise ultimately weakened the anti-Trident movement in Scotland, though Brian Quail, joint secretary for SCND, believed that campaigns before the 'Basic Case' strategy assisted the public in understanding individual systems and their unique capabilities.[24] The policy's controversy was therefore balanced between either being too academic or desperately generalised. However, the inadequacy of the 'Basic Case' strategy and any complications it produced may have been exaggerated as Michael Foot emphasised that 'campaigns for nuclear disarmament show a familiar pattern; they may rise suddenly to the highest pitch of excitement, but

---

Furthermore, women activists were often arrested during protests. Byrne, *The Campaign for Nuclear Disarmament*, p. 55.

[22] M. Morton, The Politics of Trident, *Radical Scotland*, February/March 1986, p. 9. *Radical Scotland* was a one-off edition intended to assume the role of Crann Tara magazine. Kevin Dunion relaunched *RS* in 1982, created because of the loss of national self-confidence in the devolution project following the referendum in 1978. It represented the strand of left nationalist; maxi devolutionist approach to self-government. The last issue was in 1991. Interview with Kevin Dunion, former editor for *Radical Scotland*, (23/04/03)

[23] Byrne, *The Campaign for Nuclear Disarmament*, p. 150.

[24] Interview with Helen Steven, Iona Community, (04/03/03) and Brian Quail, joint secretary for the SCND, (03/06/03).

then relapse into a seeming slothfulness.'[25] Furthermore, with the Soviet Union's invasion of Afghanistan in 1979, the assignment of 900 SS-20s to Europe and the installation of Cruise and Pershing missiles to Western Europe, it was highly improbable that any campaign, regardless of the extent of public support, was capable of preventing the Thatcher government's replacement of Polaris.

Because first delivery of Trident missiles to Scotland would not arrive until sometime in the 1990s, and all four Vanguard class boats were not scheduled to appear at Faslane until mid-1999, the disarmament movement attempted to sustain public awareness in the interim by maintaining its resistance to Polaris and producing a vast assortment of publications that addressed controversial topics such as the economic, environmental or safety-related implications of Trident.[26] Greenpeace UK produced several publications such as *The UK's Involvement in the Naval Nuclear Arms Race* in 1987, *Naval Nuclear Bases: The Costs to the Clyde* in July 1988 and *The Problems of the Trident Programme* in July 1991, all of which considered the economic burden of Trident to the British taxpayer or the probability and effects of a serious nuclear accident in a naval reactor or nuclear weapon on the Clyde.[27] Numerous CND publications similar to Malcolm Dando and Paul Rodgers's *The Death of Deterrence* also offered information pertaining to Trident's offensive capabilities while the SCND established monthly instalments of *Scottish CND News* in May 1983, which later went on to become *Nuclear Free Scotland* sometime in 1988.[28] Articles such as *US Trident in Scotland: New Evidence, Scotland United Against Trident* and *Trash Trident: Bin the Bomb* made for

---

[25] Foot, *Dr. Strangelove, I Presume*, p. 187.

[26] HMS *Vanguard* arrived in October 1992, HMS *Victorious* in May 1994, HMS *Vigilant* in March 1996 and HMS *Vengeance* in May 1999.

[27] See The UK's Involvement in the Naval Nuclear Arms Race, (London: Greenpeace UK, 1987), Naval Nuclear Bases: The Costs to the Clyde, (London: Greenpeace UK, July 1988) and Problems of the Trident Programme, (London: Greenpeace UK, 1991).

[28] Dando and Rodgers discussed Trident's capabilities, which made it possible for one country to destroy an opponent's command and control systems and arsenal in a first-strike. Malcolm Dando and Paul Rodgers, *The Death of Deterrence*, (London: CND Publications, 1984), and interview with J. Ainslie, head administrator SCND (25/03/03).

common literature within this Scottish periodical, and addressed the modernisation of the US deterrent in the Holy Loch, argued that '70 per cent of Scots remain opposed to Trident' or questioned the utility of the system.[29] In order to address the concerns of employees in the defence industry the SCND, in collaboration with the Scottish Trades Union Congress (STUC), also released *Trident in Scotland: Not Safe, Not Economic, Not Wanted* in 1994, arguing that 'resources freed by axing Trident could be applied to rebuilding our crumbling infrastructure, improving public services, and supporting diversification in the military industrial complex.'[30] Finally, published by the SCND, comprehensive documents such as February 1994's *The Safety of Trident: An Assessment of the Radiation Risks Associated with the UK Trident Programme* addressed a number of environmental issues while March 1999's *Trident: Britain's Weapon of Mass Destruction* discussed the threat of Trident in the post-Cold War era.[31] Though this was merely a reasonable sample of the materials produced, several of these documents were strategically placed to coincide with the arrival or operation of Trident SSBNs.[32]

National and Scottish CND were also diligent in emphasising the findings of both the 1990 Drell Commission and the 1992 Oxburgh Report, which ultimately highlighted the technical difficulties Trident was experiencing in its developmental stages. In mid-1990, the Drell Report raised serious concerns about the design of the missile with scientific experts believing the missile should have been subjected to an immediate national policy review as Trident featured an explosive

---

[29] US Trident in Scotland: New Evidence, *Scottish CND News*, August-September 1987, p. 6, Scotland United Against Trident, *Nuclear Free Scotland*, June 1992, p. 1, and Trash Trident: Bin the Bomb, *Nuclear Free Scotland*, April 1996 p. 3.

[30] *Trident in Scotland: Not Safe, Not Economic, Not Wanted*, (Glasgow: STUC and SCND, 1994), p. 23.

[31] *Trident in Scotland: Not Safe, Not Economic, Not Wanted*, (Glasgow: STUC and SCND, 1994), p. 23.

[32] Ploughshares produced the *Trident Ploughshares: Tri-denting It Handbook* 'The Pledge to Prevent Nuclear Crime' said it was the duty of every citizen to uphold the law relating to nuclear weapons and that all should work to carefully, safely and peacefully disarm any weapon that breaches humanitarian law. *Tri-denting it*, (Norfolk: Trident Ploughshares, 1999), p. 91.

propellant that 'could be accidentally detonated'.[33] When the Defence Committee questioned the Ministry of Defence concerning the implications these problems presented for the British system, the Ministry stated that it could not release any information relating to the design of the American warhead.[34] Furthermore, in July 1992 the Government also agreed to appoint a new nuclear weapons safety watchdog after the chief scientific adviser to the Ministry of Defence expressed concern that budget and manpower cuts could affect safety. The Second Report from the Defence Committee only explained that the Oxburgh Report recommended that the nuclear weapon safety champion have the competence, resources and seniority to discharge a large number of responsibilities.[35] Though the facts are unclear, several improvements were made and revisions in safety guidelines did take place. Drell, Oxburgh and restricted access to information pertaining to matters of national security intensified the disarmament movement's concerns with Trident, but more importantly, pressure from groups like SCND provided an extra incentive for the Ministry of Defence to uphold, and even improve, safety practices concerning the UK deterrent.

While full-blown demonstrations were vital in expressing public dissatisfaction with Trident, stringent economic guidelines and geographic location certainly encouraged the disarmament movement to be conservative in its use of such activities in Scotland. Based on previous experiences mass demonstrations outside of London were unlikely to 'draw more than 30,000 people' despite the fact that there was considerable agitation by activists in Scotland to mount more events outside of London.[36] Though demonstrations held in Hyde Park from 1981–1983 attracted roughly 250,000 to 400,000 per event, the suggested figure for demonstrations in Scotland was upheld when in April 1982 Ian Leitch and SCAT organised rallies in Glasgow and

---

[33] M. Evans, 'Trident safety doubts raised', *The Times*, 20 December 1990, p. 2.
[34] Eighth Report from the Defence Committee, *The Progress of the Trident Programme*, HC 286 of Session 1990-91, p. 9.
[35] Second Report from the Defence Committee, *The Progress of the Trident Programme*, HC 297 of Session 1993-94, p. 19.

Dundee with police estimates placing the turnout at roughly 10,000 while conflicting reports estimated attendance to be in the neighbourhood of 30,000.[37] The SCND further organised concerts, marches, rallies and vigils at Faslane, Glasgow, Dundee, and Helensburgh to correspond with the October 1992 arrival of the first of the Vanguard class.[38] However, the *Glasgow Herald* described the event in Helensburgh as 'an uneventful passage to Faslane for the Vanguard at the conclusion of her voyage from the builder's yard' as several 'hundred' people gathered at the shoreline.[39] With limited access to the necessary economic and human resources, and serious implications unavoidably linked to the public's participation, both the CND and SCND recognised that smaller demonstrations in Scotland were detrimental to the disarmament movement's cause and consequently reinterpreted these efforts as either actions or blockades to compensate for the lower attendance figures.

Though actions and blockades relied heavily on an activist's willingness to participate in some form of non-violent direct action, and thus be at greater risk of arrest, the decision to conduct flurries of these activities after the arrival of Trident in 1992 often provided the necessary media exposure in which the disarmament movement could broadcast its message of unilateral disarmament. Since the arrival of Polaris in the 1960s these operations encompassed an assortment of tactics that included spontaneous presentations, bonfires, premeditated interruption of submarines while navigating through Scottish lochs and the blockading of

---

[36] Byrne, The Campaign for Nuclear Disarmament, p. 167.

[37] Events were supported by the Tory Reform Group, the Quakers, CND local groups and members from the Labour movement. A. Campbell, 'Church silence over Trident condemned', *Glasgow Herald*, 12 April 1982, p. 4, and Byrne, *The Campaign for Nuclear Disarmament*, p. 167.

[38] The arrival of the first boat was expected to draw considerable support for the movement but failed to generate the same figures as Polaris in 1961. Interview with J. Ainslie, head administrator of SCND, (25/03/03).

[39] C. Gordon, 'Anti-Trident protestors brushed aside at Faslane', *Glasgow Herald*, 26 October 1996, p. 2. For more see S. Houston, 'Four arrests as Trident comes home', *Greenock Telegraph*, 26 October 1992, p. 1, C. Page, 'Four held in Clyde demo', *Greenock Telegraph*, 25 May 1994, p. 1, and H. Reilly, 'Third Trident makes debut at Clyde Base: CND protesters sail out to meet sub', *The Lennox Herald*, 29 March 1996, p. 9.

Faslane itself or warhead transports. While the act of spray painting slogans like 'Ban Trident' upon the public entrance to the Palace of Westminster or a bonfire action at Faslane with a mock Trident submarine set alight outside the base hardly amused law enforcement, these exercises demonstrated the intensity of deep-seated emotions many activists associated with the Trident presence. Attempts to physically disrupt the patrols of 16,000 tonne SSBNs while they traversed the Clyde also became a featured item for the disarmament movement as countless numbers of activists, with little regard for their own personal safety, attempted to swim into the path of these submarines after their systematic arrival to the Gare Loch. Furthermore, the blockading of Faslane had been accompanied by a multitude of operations that included activists chaining themselves to rails, damaging fences that surrounded Coulport or Faslane and frequent incidents of illegal trespass. While these actions were usually conducted in the west of Scotland, the disarmament movement's interference with Trident warhead convoys occurred throughout the wider UK.[40]

After 1992 the transport of Trident warheads and the deliberate interruption of such convoys were topics of discussion that deserved undivided attention. Over the course of their journey, two Trident warheads were placed into special containers and transported to Coulport within a specially articulated Truck Cargo Heavy-Duty Mark 2 (TCHD Mk2) vehicle. Four to six police motorcyclists, along with Ministry of Defence and civilian police, then escorted these vehicles with convoys being anywhere from three to five TCHD Mk2s travelling at a gross weight of forty-eight tonnes at fifty miles per hour.[41] These convoys, plus escort, transported warheads from Aldermaston on a

[40] In the US almost 600 arrest citations were also issued at a transmitter site for the American Trident system in Wisconsin since 1991, and people who have refused to cooperate with sentencing have served a combined total of more than 5 years in county jail. Interview with John LaForge, Nukewatch US, (13/03/03).

[41] In July 1999 Doug Henderson, Armed Forces Minister, announced that responsibility for the routine movement of nuclear weapons within the UK was transferred from the RAF to the Ministry of Defence Police. Ministry of Defence, Press Release: *Transfer of nuclear convoy responsibilities*, 15 July 1999.

monthly basis and normally passed London on the M25, took the M1/A1 to Newcastle, then travelled either west to the A74 or north around Edinburgh with all warheads escorted through the centre of Glasgow on the M8.[42] To the dissatisfaction of the disarmament movement, since the transport of Polaris warheads, these convoys occasionally experienced mechanical failures. To limit 'unscheduled stops', in mid-March 1994 the Ministry of Defence spent an estimated £60,000 modifying its fleet of transports to end an embarrassing series of roadside breakdowns.[43] These modifications did nothing to reverse the disarmament movement's aversion to motorway warhead deliveries. Nukewatch UK, which monitored the movements of nuclear convoys throughout the country, worked with groups like Faslane Peace Camp and Ploughshares on numerous occasions to stop the transport of these weapons.[44] Of the numerous Polaris or Trident convoys, in September 1996, one convoy was actually stopped five times near a housing estate in Balloch near Loch Lomond while two activists cut through security fencing and managed to disable a transport vehicle held at Cambridgeshire's RAF Wittering in November 1999.[45] Despite the fact that the Health and Safety Executive emphasised that nuclear weapons

---

[42] SCND, *The Safety of Trident*, p. 18.

[43] The first Trident convoy to suffer mechanical failure was on the M62 in July 1992, and by May 1993 another convoy was halted for four hours near the Erskine Bridge outside Glasgow. Information is freely available from the SCND website, and incidents also concerned SCND due to the events of 11 September 2001. D. Fairhall, 'N-warhead trucks grind to a halt', *The Guardian*, 17 March 1994, p. 6. And J. Ainslie, *The Safety of Trident*, p. 18.

[44] Nukewatch UK was concerned with the complete elimination of these transports as well as the decommissioning of Trident, not just issues of safety. Interview with Jane Tallents, Nukewatch UK, (06/03/03). In 1982 the Peace Camp accumulated just thirty-five arrests. By February 1997 the camp amassed well over 1,200 arrests ranging from offences involving the destruction of Ministry of Defence property to the disruption of warhead transports through its vast network of contacts with the international movement. *Faslane Peace Camp – list of actions*, http://dspace.dial.pipex.com/cndscot/camp/arrests.htm.(02/03/03).

[45] RAF Wittering was an air force station in Cambridgeshire. Zelter, *Trident on Trial*, p. 52. Interruptions were numerous. In October 1996 activists were arrested in Balloch as they stopped a convoy that experienced mechanical failure as it ascended a hill en route to Helensburgh. In November 1998 a convoy was stopped twice by activists as it passed through Rhu on the shores of the Gare Loch and at Whistlefield roundabout near Coulport. *Trident Convoy stopped in Dumbarton*, Available: www.banthebomb.org/news/90612a.htm (01/07/02) *Nuclear Convoy stopped*, Available: www.banthebomb.org/news961010.htm (01/07/02).

must be transported in a way that complies with International Atomic Energy Agency (IAEA) guidelines, the transportation of explosives alongside radioactive material was contrary to British regulations due to an exemption clause for 'instruments of war'.[46] The Ministry of Defence was able to evade successfully IAEA policies but the disarmament movement's persistence eventually brought international law to the forefront of the Trident debate.

While moral principles arguing against the act of nuclear deterrence were incorporated into the policies of the disarmament movement since the early 1960s, in 1983 SCRAM also cited the standards of the Nuremberg Tribunal that ruled under international law against the 'planning, preparing, initiating, or waging a war of aggression'.[47] By 1984 the CND Annual Conference also endorsed a motion that committed it to put greater emphasis on the legality question of nuclear weapons in the future.[48] This legal strategy, a tactic not exploited by the anti-Polaris campaign, proved unexpectedly successful for the anti-Trident movement. In July 1996 the International Court of Justice (ICJ) issued its controversial decision that it could find no circumstances in which the threat or use of nuclear weapons would not violate humanitarian law. While this ruling was regarded as a symbolic gesture by the governments of nuclear-weapon states, the disarmament movement's interpretation of this verdict was in no way dismissive.

It must be understood that from 1996 the ICJ decision had significant influence over the strategies of the disarmament movement, with the Scottish legal system offering considerable discomfort to the Blair government by October 1999. It is well documented that during a Ploughshares action in early June 1999, activists Angela Zelter, Anne Moxley and Ulla Roder boarded a Ministry of Defence barge, a floating laboratory that monitored the magnetic, acoustic, thermal, radar and visual signals that Trident submarines produced, and destroyed property

---

[46] SCND, *The Safety of Trident*, p. 23.
[47] D. Lowe, 'Factors that defused the Trident Inquiry', *The Glasgow Herald*, 27 June 1983.
[48] Byrne, *The Campaign for Nuclear Disarmament*, p. 145.

worth an estimated £80,000.[49] Taking comfort from the guidelines provided by international law, they remained incarcerated after being placed into custody because they would only accept bail on the understanding that disarmament activity would not be considered to be a crime by the Scottish court. When the Greenock Sheriff Court trial commenced on 27 September 1999 a defence of necessity was pushed forward which argued that although the women had been wilful, they had not been malicious.[50] After a trial of twenty-four days the defence managed to convince Sheriff Margaret Gimblett on 20 October 1999 that:

> The three accused took the view that if it was illegal, and given the horrendous nature of nuclear weapons, that they had an obligation in terms of international law, never mind morally to do the little they could do to stop ... the deployment and use of nuclear weapons in a situation which could be construed as a threat.[51]

In the midst of great controversy Trident's legitimacy was formally challenged as Gimblett instructed the jury to acquit, thus validating the thirty-eight years of protest in Scotland. While reactions from NATO, the US government or other nuclear-weapons states remained unclear, the decision must have distressed the British political establishment as

---

[49] Zelter, *Trident on Trial*, p. 54.

[50] The Procurator Fiscal charged that they (1) maliciously and wilfully damaged the vessel *Maytime*; (2) attempted to steal two inflatable life rafts; (3) maliciously and wilfully damaged equipment on board *Maytime*; and (4) maliciously and wilfully damaged equipment by depositing it 'in the waters of Loch Goil, whereby said items became waterlogged, useless and inoperable'. The Defence further offered five expert witnesses, including Professor Francis Boyle, University of Illinois, who testified that *Trident* could not be used in a lawful manner; Judge Ulf Panzer fro m Germany, who gave evidence of the legitimacy of non-violent action to uphold the law; Professor Paul Rogers, Bradford University, who discussed the capabilities of the *Trident* system, the imminent danger of nuclear war and of the effectiveness of civil resistance to change official policies; Professor Jack Boag, who gave evidence about the associated dangers of nuclear weapons; and Rebecca Johnston of ACRONYM, Geneva, who explained the consequences of the failure of successive UK governments to fulfil its obligations to disarm under the Non-Nuclear Proliferation Treaty (NNPT). Each submitted that international law applied in Scotland, that the threat or use of nuclear weapons was found to be generally contrary to international law by the International Court of Justice and the deployment of Trident was clearly interpreted as a threat.

former Conservative minister, Lord Mackay of Ardbrecknish, proclaimed 'that pretty well anyone can walk into a nuclear installation related to Trident and do more or less what they want.'[52] Needless to say, the British media had a field day. Forced to react, the Blair government set into motion a rare legal process in Scotland referred to as a Lord Advocate's Reference, which would later prevent other judges from providing similar acquittals.[53] Despite the obvious humiliation that the Greenock trial provided, Labour's embarrassment also stemmed from the relationships Michael Foot and Neil Kinnock established with the disarmament movement during their stints as party leaders.

According to naval historian Jim Ring, the CND had established a long running relationship with Labour as the party was 'well stocked with members of CND' who had 'from the first publicly opposed the Nassau agreement.'[54] While relationships between the disarmament movement and parties like the SNP, the Scottish Socialist Party and the Green Party were relatively straightforward, over the course of two decades the same could not be said for the rapport between Labour and CND. In 1987 Hillary Wainwright, freelance writer and researcher, explained that:

> The Labourist left, as well as right, have assumed Britain's role as a 'world leader' in all their international campaigns. In the early years of CND (1957–63) they [Labour] presumed that this greatness could be deployed 'by example' to bring about world peace. It is a stance which is not only an arrogant fantasy but is also, in the end, self imploding ... If Britain gives up her weapons, she gives up the only basis on which she remains a world power.[55]

---

[51] Zelter, *Trident on Trial*, p.69.

[52] *Nuclear Safeguards Bill*, Lords Hansard, Col. 779 Vol. 45, 30 November 1999.

[53] Zelter, *Trident on Trial*, p. 79.

[54] Labour CND, composed of Labour Party members and an organising executive that was Britain-wide, also had beginnings that dated back to the earliest days of Polaris. Interview with Dr. Jim Taggart, Labour CND, (08/02/03). J. Ring, *We Come Unseen: The Untold Story of Britain's Cold War Submariners*, (London: John Murray Publishers, 2001), p. 55.

Far from enthusiastic with this relationship, Wainwright went on to state that 'one independent movement which has upset the Labour Party's equilibrium is the peace movement.'[56] By the early 1980s only a few Cabinet members had previously been members of the CND with its influence on the party significant yet intermittent.[57] Prior to the 1979 General Election Labour Prime Minister James Callaghan had quietly secured a deal with the Carter administration for the UK to acquire Trident. However, during the 1983 and 1987 General Elections Foot and Kinnock pledged to scrap Trident. Kinnock reversed party policy in 1990 and Tony Blair opted to continue with a system that was virtually complete after defeating left-wing demands to decommission Trident in 1995.[58] Although there were other considerations, Blair was unprepared to dismantle a system that maintained thousands of jobs in Scotland. Hoping to somehow persuade Labour to reconsider, in June 1997 the SCND submitted to the Blair government 'Submission to the Strategic Defence Review from the Scottish Campaign for Nuclear Disarmament' to influence Labour's 'Strategic Defence Review White Paper', a document that ultimately failed to meet the disarmament movement's expectations.[59] Though the disarmament movement was successful in encouraging Scottish Labour to maintain a policy of unilateral nuclear disarmament following the resurrection of the Scottish Parliament, John

---

[55] H. Wainwright, *Labour: The Tale of Two Parties*, (London: The Hargoath Press, 1987), p. 81.
[56] ibid. p. 274.
[57] Foot, *Dr Strangelove, I Presume*, p. 72 and Byrne, *The Campaign for Nuclear Disarmament*, p. 147.
[58] In 1983 Callaghan declared the unilateral disarmament a dead issue for the British electorate. J. Ring, *We Come Unseen*, p. 151. Union delegates voted by 44.2 per cent to 55.8 per cent against a call to reaffirm the 1993 and 1994 conference decisions to scrap Trident as an essential step towards the elimination of nuclear weapons. J. Copely, 'Labour Party Conference: Unions back Blair's pleas to keep Trident', *The Telegraph*, 5 October 1995, p. 7.
[59] The submission contained five points which argued that Scots rejected the utility of Trident and that the UK government should cancel the programme. J. Ainslie, *Submission to the Strategic Defence Review from the Scottish Campaign for Nuclear Disarmament*, 27 June 1997. The Labour government began its Strategic Defence Review (SDR) in May of 1997 and was published on 8 July 1998. As declared in the Labour election manifesto it affirmed the Government's commitment to maintaining a nuclear deterrent but made a number of changes to it. T. Dodd and Mark Oakes, *The Strategic Defence Review White Paper, International affairs and defence section*, Cmd. Paper 3999, 1998, p. 31-36.

McAllion, Labour Party MP for Dundee East, explained that, 'only British action can further the cause for scrapping Trident … unilateralist Scottish action could merely move it along the coast, never get rid of it.'[60] Despite this loss, Labour's decision to maintain the UK deterrent did little to discourage the efforts of the disarmament movement.

Scots protesting at Abermarle near Newcastle-upon-Tyne against lorries carrying Trident nuclear warheads to Scotland. *(© Scottish Campaign for Nuclear Disarmament)*

Obstacles for the Anti-Trident Movement

Besides overcoming the erratic nature of public support, the disarmament movement was inevitably forced to confront substantial

---

[60] *John McAllion: Nationalism and Identity.* Available: http://www.sol.co.uk/j/jmcallion/cl.htm. (01/07/02).

political opposition, media bias, a sagging economy and public indifference if it hoped someday to encourage the decommissioning of Trident. Because the Thatcher government inherited its relationship with the disarmament movement it 'adopted the same strategy as its predecessors towards the peace movement', ignored it when possible, and, 'when pressed', dismissed 'its arguments as unrealistic' and concentrated 'on presenting the case for replacing Polaris with Trident.'[61] The behaviour of activists in Scotland after July 1980 encouraged the latter. In January 1983 the Conservative government employed extreme tactics when it appointed Michael Heseltine as Minister of Defence with a 'mission to counter CND influence', allowing for 'a well-funded anti-CND propaganda unit' to monitor its activities.[62] This fierce form of political opposition included a multi-million pound national advertising campaign accentuating the necessity of the British nuclear deterrent and the establishment of Defence Secretariat 19 (D.S. 19), a special unit inside the Ministry of Defence which methodically depicted the CND as left-wing extremists prepared to jeopardise national security.[63] Heseltine's aggressive initiatives provoked CND to claim that there had been interference with its mail along with telephone-tapping operations, which the Home Secretary would neither 'confirm nor deny'.[64] Though the CND pressed for a full inquiry the issue was overshadowed by Clive Ponting's supposed breaching of the Official Secrets Act, leaving CND exposed to an unspecified number of operations and allowing the Thatcher government greater freedom in its attempts to influence public opinion.[65]

---

[61] Byrne, *The Campaign for Nuclear Disarmament*, p. 147.

[62] *Campaign for Nuclear Disarmament*. Available: www.cnduk.org. (02/07/02).

[63] Much of this was achieved through the media. Public Records Office, *Operational Selection Policy OSP11: Nuclear Weapons Policy 1967-1998,* Available:
http://www.pro.gov.uk/recordsmanagement/acquisition/osp11nuclear.htm, (04/03/03).

[64] Byrne, *The Campagn for Nuclear Disarmament*, p. 149.

[65] Clive Ponting was acquitted after he was accused of breaching the UK's Official Secrets Act. He had responsibility for 'the policy and political aspects of the operational activities of the Royal Navy' during 1982 Falklands war. Ponting had the job of drafting replies and answers on the sinking of the *Belgrano* by the Royal Navy on 2nd May 1982. Because he believed that the Government was deliberately misleading the Commons, a select committee and the public,

It should be noted that Heseltine later claimed that the defeat of CND was 'the proudest achievement of his political career'.[66]

Although the true extent of the surveillance by the Ministry of Defence before 1983 is unclear, it is certain that the disarmament movement's sites in proximity to military facilities were consistently monitored. In 1984 protest groups were considered a relatively new threat to the physical security of military establishments, with control of demonstrations and peace camp activity outside Ministry of Defence property deemed a matter for the civil police. However, the Ministry was naturally alert to the need 'to prevent attempts at deliberate trespass for political reasons'.[67] In April of that year Commodore David Morse reported to the Defence Committee at Faslane that a handful of permanent residents inhabited the Peace Camp, and its inhabitants fluctuated from 'four or five and up to fifty or sixty'. Furthermore, Morse explained that activists were under a certain degree of surveillance and that, 'we do know who the regulars are but there are many regulars who come for two days and some stay for a week, then the numbers build up and it is for us at that time to build up our identification.'[68] Activities surrounding Rosyth Royal Dockyard in the east of Scotland, where refitting operations for Trident submarines were to take place before being relocated south of the Border, were also under

---

he acted out of professional conscience in sending two documents to Tam Dalyell MP. The documents got to the Chairman of the select committee on Foreign Affairs, who, in turn, gave them back to the Secretary of State at the Ministry of Defence. Ponting was then prosecuted for breach of sec. 2(1)(a) of the Official Secrets Act. See C. Ponting, *The Right to Know. The inside story of the Belgrano affair*, (London: Sphere Books) 1985.

[66] Foot, *Dr Strangelove I Presume*, p. 76.

[67] In 1984 the Defence Committee explained that 'protest groups currently account for the great majority of unauthorised incursions into military establishments' and that 'these incursions have posed no real threat to the physical security of those establishments but the authorities have had to meet the nuisance caused by their activities by a variety of countermeasures'. Second Report from the Defence Committee, *The Physical Security of Military Installations in the United Kingdom*, HC 397-II of Session 1983–1984, p. vii.

[68] The Ministry of Defence was responsible for the physical security of several thousand sites. Physical security fell into five broad categories that included 'innocent trespass, criminal entry, espionage, protest groups, terrorist attack/sabotage'. Second Report from the Defence Committee, *The Physical Security of Military Installations in the United Kingdom*, HC 397-I of Session 1983-1984, p. 43.

regular observation.[69] On 1 May 1984 at HM Naval Base Rosyth the Defence Committee heard evidence from Chief Constable W. Moodie, Fife Constabulary, who explained that authorities 'maintained a low profile approach to this particular matter and ... the activities of those people whilst they were located in the area were monitored.'[70] Though incomparable to the practices of D.S. 19, after the Trident programme assumed the principal burden of providing deterrence with the arrival of HMS *Vigilant,* disarmament actions were augmented and the Ministry of Defence sustained a credible level of surveillance.[71]

Along with these developments, the loss of Strathclyde Regional Council's support forced Faslane Peace Camp to confront increasing hostilities from Argyll and Bute Council after the reorganisation of local government in 1996. According to one peace camper, 'when borders changed', the camp's relationship with an 'anti-nuclear Council' was replaced by 'the animosities of a pro-nuclear Council'.[72] Conservative Councillor Billy Petrie argued that local people wanted the authority to reclaim the property, and by April 1997 activists vowed to fight a decision by the Council to bulldoze the area. After the arrival of eviction papers in April 1998, campers challenged the validity and competence of the eviction as the lease in question, which gave activists and Strathclyde Regional Council the right to exercise a one month termination clause, contained an unwritten agreement that the site was available to activists so long as nuclear weapons existed at the base. Although campers lived in mobile homes, legal representation for the camp also claimed the activists had security of tenure under the Housing (Scotland) Act 1987. While the

---

[69] In 1984 Rosyth Royal Dockyard was chosen to perform though this responsibility was transferred to Devonport after 1993.

[70] Second Report from the Defence Committee, *The Physical Security of Military Installations in the United Kingdom,* HC 397-I of Session 1983-1984. p. 71.

[71] Faslane was the centre of controversy in 1984 when the words, 'Vermin, Vermin, Vermin' were supposedly used to signal the suspected intrusion of the base by Faslane Peace Campers. '"Vermin" alarm tag-base deny shame', *Helensburgh Advertiser,* 2 March 1984, p. 1. Statement on Defence Estimates 1996, Presented to Parliament by the Secretary of State for Defence by Command of Her Majesty, *Chapter Four: The Defence Equipment Programme,* (London: HMSO, May 1996).

[72] Interview with Graham X, Faslane Peace Camp, (12/03/03).

loss of Britain's longest running peace camp would have compromised the efforts of the disarmament movement, at least on a temporary basis, activists rejoiced when attempts by Argyll and Bute Council to evict the campers ended in humiliation after the eviction writ was ruled incompetent. Left to perform its usual operations, the site's activities were still closely scrutinised.

While extreme political opposition and direct surveillance did little to encourage public interest in Trident or its operations, employment opportunities provided by the UK deterrent did nothing whatsoever to assist protest groups. Furthermore, a significant proportion of defence industry employees understood that the disarmament movement's position on Trident ultimately threatened thousands of jobs in Scotland. In 1984 Fife Regional Council emphasised that 'civilian employment at Rosyth naval complex represented up to 25 per cent of all employment' in the Dunfermline Employment Office area.[73] Though Rosyth Royal Dockyard was chosen to perform refits on Polaris submarines in 1963, by July 1979 the area was still home to 3,134 jobless and increasing to over 3,500 unemployed by August 1980.[74] By 1981 the economic situation still had not improved as the male unemployment rate in Dunfermline and Inverkeithing was at 8.1 percent, with Cowdenbeath's rate of unemployment at a staggering 20.4 per cent.[75] In the west of Scotland, the Strathclyde region had lost 154,000 jobs since 1979, of which 134,000 had been in the industrial sector.[76] Dumbarton itself was only one of nineteen District Councils that served the region of Strathclyde, with the unemployment rate for the area at 17.9 per cent in 1981.[77] By February 1983 unemployment figures in areas like the Vale

---

[73] The naval complex included Rosyth Royal Dockyard and Rosyth Naval Base. Rosyth Naval Base Trade Union, *Giving the Royal Dockyards a Chance: A consultative document for government, the community management and unions*, December 1984, p. 3.

[74] 'Wanted urgently: 3,500 jobs', *Dunfermline Press*, 1 August 1980, p. 5.

[75] 'Unemployment rate "appalling"', *Dunfermline Press*, 27 February 1981, p. 11.

[76] The Alternative Employment Study Group, *Polaris and Trident: The Myths and Realities of Employment*, 1985, p. 14.

[77] A total of 5,432 people were unemployed in Dumbarton with the depression particularly severe in Alexandria, Dumbarton and Renton. I. MacDonald, *Faslane Facts and Feelings: A*

of Leven, Dumbarton and Helensburgh were over 6,700.[78] With unemployment in Scotland at 14.8 per cent in 1987, the disarmament movement's dialogue on Trident hardly inspired civil unrest as its stance on nuclear weapons provided a conflict of interests for major unions and a significant proportion of the working class.

If the disarmament movement hoped to capitalise from Scottish uneasiness with nuclear weapons, it first needed to present credible employment alternatives. According to the Church of Scotland's Iain O. MacDonald, in 1981 two civilian employees of Faslane expressed that 'a lot of men' wished the jobs offered near Helensburgh were 'other than for a nuclear military base'.[79] More recently Robert Purdie, Faslane shop steward, supported this assumption when he explained that while many were comfortable in maintaining the UK's nuclear deterrent, there was also a credible number of employees who would have preferred another line of work.[80] Mary Kaldor, then University of Sussex Research Fellow at the Science Policy Research Centre Unit, explained that 'disarmament efforts are aimed at the role of armaments as objects of use' and believed that it was necessary 'to change the military-industrial culture which created them'.[81]

To meet this challenge the CND chose Barrow-in-Furness as the site of its annual demonstration in 1984, and emphasised the capital-intensive nature of nuclear weapons production while applying the STUC's argument that a shift to non-nuclear defence could actually generate greater employment. By declaring itself as an advocate for conversion, both the CND and SCND emphasised that utilising skills and resources in nuclear weapons production should be geared towards

---

study of people's knowledge and attitudes, (Edinburgh: S.R.T. project, Church of Scotland, 1981), p. 11.

[78] '1,068 out of work in town', *Helensburgh Advertiser*, 10 February 1984, p. 5.

[79] I. O. Macdonald, *Faslane Facts and Feelings*, A Study of People's Knowledge and attitudes, Edinburgh: SRT Project, Church of Scotland, 1981) p. 13.

[80] Interview with Robert Purdie, Faslane shop steward, 2 April 2003.

[81] M. Kaldor, The Armament Process in Reverse, (Ed.) E. P. Thompson and Dan Smith, *Protest and Survive*, (Middlesex: Penguin Books, 1980), p. 215.

new, socially useful production.[82] Furthermore, after the centre-section of a proto-type Trident submarine was transported to Dounreay in June 1985 a 3,000 strong march from Glasgow city centre held a four-minute silence observed in recognition of jobs 'which did not exist for young people because of expenditure on nuclear weapons programmes'.[83] However, though SCND believed the cancellation of Trident in 1994 still would be capable of creating 55,000 direct and 19,000 indirect jobs through the STUC's Emergency Jobs Package, its arguments generally failed to encourage employees of Coulport, Faslane or Rosyth Royal Dockyard to reject a reliable source of employment.[84]

Though the disarmament movement also sought to utilise the broadcast and print media in attempts to spread its message of unilateral disarmament, this relationship brought about certain advantages but was at times characterised by an element of awkwardness. Glasgow University Media Group's *War and Peace News* examined television news coverage of CND demonstrations in 1985 and commented that:

It becomes easy for opponents to depict this as an emotional movement rather than a reasoned opposition containing people who are at best well meaning but naïve, and at worst subversives playing on the fears of the population.[85]

Television also appeared to disregard the principal reasons for protest and focused more on personalities. This form of attentiveness at times adopted a vicious tenor within the print media, occasionally propagating the harmful stereotypes of peace activists as either misinformed radicals or social undesirables. In April 1983 a *Glasgow Herald* headline read 'Clyde peace convoy draws low turnout', with the SCND group travelling to Coulport in defiance of Polaris chastised for

---

[82] Byrne, *The Campaign for Nuclear Disarmament*, p. 147.
[83] The proto-type was complete with a nuclear reactor. I. Gray, 'Kent spells out CND priority', *Glasgow Herald*, 3 June 1985, p. 5.
[84] See *Trident in Scotland: Not Safe, Not Economic, Not Wanted*, p. 24.
[85] Glasgow University Media Group, *War and Peace News*, (Milton Keynes Philadelphia: OUP, 1985), p. 217.

its less than spectacular numbers. Because 'less than 200 people', many of whom who were 'unemployed', had 'little access to cars' it was argued that this was a 'poor excuse for the low turn out'.[86] However, this single example paled in comparison to other more provocative depictions. In January 1998 Graham Stewart of *The Independent* reported that the son of a nuclear submarine force commander who campaigned for disarmament wanted to follow in his father's footsteps after 'he was drawn into the CND in his mid-teens and indoctrinated by campaigners who used to give him cannabis.' The article closed on a more sinister note by stating that 'he felt he was used, then discarded by political protesters who were trying to target his father.'[87] While these representations contradicted Byrne's portrayal of the CND's social composition, damage caused to the disarmament movement by such examples was immeasurable.[88]

Despite the production of countless documents and unremitting protest actions, the disarmament movement was often forced to cope with a significant degree of public disinterest and/or ignorance on issues pertaining to either the Polaris or Trident systems. At the end of 1987 the final signing of the Intermediate-Range Nuclear Forces Treaty (INF) eliminated an entire class of US Cruise and Pershing missiles and Soviet SS-20s from Eastern and Western Europe, 'with many in Scotland under the impression that the UK's deterrent was included in this agreement'.[89] Additionally, support for the disarmament movement generally declined with the collapse of the Soviet Union in the early 1990s, along with Gorbachev's reforms, creating a relaxed atmosphere within the international community that allowed people to feel more secure. For those citizens who occasionally took notice of developments with either

---

[86] 'Clyde peace convoy draws low turn out', *Glasgow Herald*, 13 February 1985, p. 3

[87] G. Stewart, 'Anti-nuclear campaigner jumps ship for navy career', *The Independent*, 5 January 1998, p. 5.

[88] Despite lingering stereotypes, numerous examples were to the contrary. John Ainslie, head administrator of SCND, did not justify such classifications, as he was a former member of the Intelligence Corp in Northern Ireland and a minister for the Church of Scotland.

[89] J. Isaacs and T. Downing, *The Cold War*, (London: Bantam Press, 2001), p. 368. Interview with Helen Steven, Iona Community, (04/03/03).

Polaris or Trident, the withdrawal of the American fleet from the Holy Loch in late 1991 often led to confusion and the lack of an enthusiastic response from a majority of Scots to this event demonstrated the indifference most held. Though the physical presence of HMS *Vanguard* in 1992 helped the disarmament movement refocus its efforts in Scotland, the stealthy characteristics of the Trident SSBN, and its ability to remain undetected for months at a time, also assisted in undermining the efforts of groups like SCND and Ploughshares.[90] However, regardless of these mentioned impediments, both the British and international disarmament movement maintained its opposition to the UK deterrent well into the next millennium.

Conclusion

Because all fixtures of the UK's Trident deterrent were firmly in place by 1999 it is natural to discount the achievements of the disarmament movement in Scotland. Both the Thatcher government's decision to acquire Trident and the arrival of HMS *Vanguard* in 1992 failed to inspire mass rallies or monumental demonstrations and marches as Polaris had some three decades earlier. While the presence of the land-based Cruise system detracted considerably from the anti-Trident movement in the early 1980s, the arrival of the US Polaris fleet in 1961 met considerable opposition north of the Border because it was the first time many Scots experienced first-hand the extreme temperatures of a Cold War world. However, the negative impact of Trident on civil society was inevitably compromised as the Scottish public grew accustomed to the presence of such weapons over the course of thirty years. Because of this most unique familiarisation the disarmament movement's ability to draw public support, despite countless actions and blockades, significantly receded. It could also be argued that numerous publications attempting to inspire public reaction fell short of achieving

---

[90] Because the submarine platform operated at sea its presence was less obvious to both its enemies and, unlike Cruise, to those who lived in proximity to the deterrent. Interview with Helen Steven, Iona Community, (04/03/03).

their objectives, though this was not the sole purpose of such works. The implications of Cold War thaw were made obvious by the early 1990s and interest in the Trident debate was further diminished by 1999 with the disarmament movement incapable of overcoming the UK deterrent's history of safe operation or its ability to provide a sense of security and considerable employment. Therefore, one must question what the disarmament movement did in fact accomplish over the course of two decades.

For those of a sceptical nature the achievements of the disarmament movement were generally overshadowed by its inadequacies and therefore much less obvious. Though it did not convince the Labour Party of the need to decommission Trident after its return to power, a credible degree of pressure was exerted by the disarmament movement as it provided an extra stimulus for both the Ministry of Defence and the Royal Navy to operate Trident under the most stringent guidelines. Due to Scotland's long standing history of ambivalence towards nuclear weaponry, any misfortunes involving the deterrent held the potential to trigger a degree of nationalism so powerful that it could have threatened the integrity of the Union. Therefore, the disarmament movement, acting as a self-appointed watchdog, kept the political establishment on its feet. The movement's sustained presence in Scotland also prevented the issue from slipping into the political twilight, both at home and abroad, with forty years of protest inspiring the creation of multinational groups like Ploughshares. Thus, actions in Scotland served as a worldwide model for resistance. However, perhaps the most remarkable accomplishment of groups like SCND was far less ostentatious. With restricted access to the necessary resources, those people who formed the backbone of the disarmament movement were able to sustain momentum by simply surviving on a diet of sheer determination. Without this one vital characteristic, the proliferation of technologically superior weapons might have remained virtually unchallenged.

Ding Dong Dollar

Chorus:

Oh ye cannae spend a dollar when ye're deid
No ye cannae spend a dollar when ye're deid
Singing, Ding Dong Dollar, everybody holler
Ye cannae spend a dollar when ye're deid

O the Yanks have just drapped anchor aff Dunoon
And they've had a civic welcome frae the toon
As they came up the measured mile
Bonnie Mary o' Argyle
Was wearing spangled drawers ablow her goon

And the publicans will a' be daein' swell
For it's jist the thing that's sure tae ring the bell
Aye the dollars they will jingle
There'll be no a lassie single
Even though they'll maybe blow us a' tae hell.

And the Clyde is sure tae prosper now they're here
Because they're chargin' one and tenpence for the beer
Ay, an' if you want a taxi
They stick it up your – jersey
An' they charge you thirty bob tae Sandbank Pier

But the Glesca Moderator disnae mind
In fact he thinks the Yanks are awfy kind
'Cause if it's Heaven that ye're goin'
It's a quicker way than rowin'
And there's sure tae be naebody left behind.

Words by (Trad/Thurso Berwick/J.Mack/Jim McLean

Trident submarine HMS *Vengeance* being launched at Barrow-in-Furness *(© Scottish Campaign for Nuclear Disarmament)*

Decommissioned SSNs and SLBMs at Rosyth from the Cold War era are a lingering source of controversy in Scotland. *(© Scottish Campaign for Nuclear Disarmament)*

Chapter 7

THE END OF THE ROAD FOR ACTION AGAINST TRIDENT?

SCOTS LAW AND THE TRIDENT PROGRAMME

Julius Komorowski

Perhaps the main feature of the Cold War was the massive stockpiling of nuclear weapons and the prospect, sometimes the imminent prospect, of nuclear conflict and holocaust. But the unfortunate truth is that with the end of the Cold War has not come the end of nuclear weapons. Trident, which is a marked expansion on its predecessor Polaris, came into operation after the Cold War had ended. Nuclear weapons such as Trident are no longer to be used to threaten rival super-powers, but as a means of exerting force and control over weaker states. It is appropriate then, that we should examine what can be done with these nuclear relics of the Cold War, so that they might join the war in the history books. For this reason a legal paper is not so out of place, for what is law if it is not the careful historical study of previous court decisions so that we might learn what might happen in the future – avoiding the repetition of previous mistakes and taking advantage of arguments that have proved successful in the courts already? Therefore, it will be necessary to consider cases from 1765 onwards, from the Napoleonic War, the First and the Second World War.

Direct Action and Resistance in the Courts

Action has been taken against nuclear weapons since they were first deployed in the 1950s. Tactics have included mass marches, sit-downs, and attempts to enter and occupy military bases. A quick survey of some reported case law illustrates the point well. *Chandler v. DPP* (1962)[2] involved an attempted occupation of a US air base where nuclear weapons were based. The accused came from the 'Committee of 100' and were given prison sentences of eighteen months and twelve months. The case is an important authority on Government military powers, and on the scope of the official secrets legislation under which they were prosecuted. *Cheney v. Conn* (1968)[3] involved a rather different tactic: a taxpayer refused to pay the portion of his taxes that would be spent on nuclear weapons arguing that it was not permissible to collect taxes for a purpose which was illegal under international law.

More recently there has been a number of cases arising from the activities of Trident Ploughshares. Trident Ploughshares is a non-violent direct action group organised around small affinity group units, acting independently of each other, and also collaborating for larger events such as mass blockades of the submarine base at Faslane. *John v. Donnelly* (1999)[4] involved an accused charged with vandalising a fence around Faslane by cutting it, and is an important authority on the meaning of the 'reasonable excuse' defence against the statutory crime of vandalism. *Smith v. Donnelly* (2001)[5] involved a sit-down protest outside Faslane and is the leading case on the crime of breach of the peace. There is also constant activity south of the border, *Hutchinson v. DPP* (2000)[6] being an example of fence cutting at Aldermaston Weapons Establishment.

---

[2] [1964] AC 763, [1962] 3 WLR 694, [1962] 3 All ER 142.

[3] [1968] 1 WLR 242, [1968] 1 All ER 779.

[4] 1999 JC 336, 2000 SLT 11, 1999 SCCR 802.

[5] 2002 JC 65, 2001 SLT 1007, 2001 SCCR 800.

[6] [2000] EWHC 67 QB. Viewable online at:
http://www.courtservice.gov.uk/judgmentsfiles/j114/queen_hutchinson.htm

Anti-nuclear cases are so pervasive that law students will come across a number of such cases in the course of ordinary study. This is because the struggle against nuclear weapons does not end with arrest but continues in the courts where important precedents are established. In one recent Scottish case the court noted that: 'it is clear that in doing what they did, the … [accused] were effectively inviting prosecution, with a view … to … perhaps inducing some members of the public to see the trial as some kind of "test case"'.[7] Recently in England activists have sought to campaign directly through the courts, applying for legal declarations that Aldermaston Weapons Establishment was acting illegally under environmental law with regard to the international legal position on nuclear weapons[8] and that war in Iraq without a Security Council resolution would be illegal.[9]

The constant threat of nuclear weapons has been met by constant resistance through various means of direct action. These have gone hand-in-hand with resistance in the courts. It is therefore very appropriate to look at possible legal justifications for direct action. To date, every case bearing on the legality of nuclear weapons has been lost with one exception: the trial of three anti-nuclear activists in Greenock Sheriff Court in 1999 who were acquitted of all charges on the basis of the defence of necessity and international law. The legal basis of this ruling was overturned by the High Court of Justiciary in Edinburgh. I will examine why the 'Trident Three' enjoyed success in Greenock only to hit a dead end in Edinburgh, and whether there are any avenues of challenge left after that decision.[10]

---

[7] *Lord Advocate's Reference (No. 1 of 2000)* 2001 JC 143, 2001 SLT, 507 2001 SCCR 296 at para. [18]. Also viewable online at: http://www.scotcourts.gov.uk/opinionsv/11_00.html

[8] *Marchiori v. Environment Agency* [2002] EWCA Civ 3, *The Independent*, 31 January 2002.

[9] *Campaign for Nuclear Disarmament v. Prime Minister* [2002] EWHC 2777, *The Times*, December 27, 2002.

[10] It is hoped that the format of this research will not be overly legalistic. It is aimed at the layperson, and is simply an introduction to the legal issues involved. Space does not allow for explanation of all legal concepts. This research is concerned with the position in Scots law. The United Kingdom has three legal systems: English law, which covers England & Wales; Northern Irish law which is based on English law; and Scots law which has different historical roots from English law. However, all the UK shares a central Government in London; the

The Trident Three – 'The Greenock Trial': *HM Advocate v. Zelter, Roder & Moxley.*

Angie Zelter,[11] Ulla Roder and Ellen Moxely were members of Trident Ploughshares. On 8 June 1999 the three travelled in a small boat and boarded the test barge *Maytime* in Loch Goil which was used to conduct research on Trident submarines. Arriving undetected, they set about committing sabotage by dumping computer equipment, fax machines and other articles into the loch, and used glue and solder to cause damage within the barge itself. In the course of attempting to board another nearby vessel they also accidentally set loose two lifeboats.

The Trident Three were prosecuted before a jury in the Sheriff Court at Greenock with causing malicious damage to items on the test barge and either damaging the lifeboats or causing them to drift away and thus stealing them. At the trial the accused did not dispute that they had damaged the equipment. The accused and the prosecutor agreed that the cost of damage was around £80,000. The accused argued that they did not have the required mental elements for the crimes, in that they didn't act maliciously and that they didn't wish to steal the lifeboats for themselves. In a legal context, these matters are not relevant. They also argued that their acts were justified by necessity and that Trident was illegal under international law, and that they were entitled to take action to stop it. They presented evidence from an expert witness on international law at the trial. The sheriff ruled that the accused could not be found guilty because of their motives and their belief in the danger and illegality posed by Trident. The jury found them not guilty as instructed by the sheriff.[12]

Houses of Parliament as a law-making body; and the House of Lords as the supreme civil court. English law and Scots law are very similar in certain areas, such as constitutional law. Scots judges often look to English law when discussing how Scots law should be developed.

[11] Readers may be interested in Angie Zelter's book: *Trident on trial: the case for people's disarmament* (Luath Press, 2001).

[12] The trial itself is unreported, but the following reviews the case: S. Neff, 'Idealism in Action: International law and nuclear weapons in Greenock Sheriff Court', *Edinburgh Law Review*, (2000), vol. 4, p. 74.

The Lord Advocate's Reference (No. 1 of 2000)[13]

As the Trident Three were found 'not guilty' after a jury trial, no court process could be used to try and reverse that verdict. However, the Lord Advocate has the power to refer legal questions arising in trials to the High Court of Justiciary for an opinion. Such action can be taken when a prosecutor loses on a legal point that the Lord Advocate thinks should be decided differently, so that it is not followed in future cases. References have occurred eight times since the procedure was created in 1975. The Lord Advocate referred to the High Court of Justiciary the question of whether it was proper to admit expert evidence. On customary international law he also questioned the circumstances under which otherwise illegal acts could be justified due to the illegal nature of something, or a person's objection to it. Despite the acquittal of the Trident Three they, nonetheless, had the right to appear before the court and argue their point of view. They argued, as they had previously done at their trial, that their acts were justified under the defence of necessity and under international law.

The International Law Defence

Any successful defence based on international law must pass three hurdles. These are: that the activity acted against is in breach of international law; that the breach of international law is recognised in Scots law; and that the breach gives rise to a defence. The High Court of Justiciary held that not every use of nuclear weapons could be said to be illegal before the event. This was because international law permits the use of weapons, even if they harm civilians, provided that the military advantage gained is proportionate.[14] It further held that there was no specific threat of the use of Trident and therefore no particular potential

---

[13] See note 7, supra.

[14] First Additional Protocol to the Geneva Conventions, 1977, Art. 51 (5): attacks that cause 'incidental loss of civilian life, [etc.]... which would be excessive in relation to the concrete and direct military advantage anticipated' are prohibited.

use to be examined; thus there was no illegal deployment of nuclear weapons at that time.[15] The respondents did not get over the first hurdle. There has, however, been much criticism of this finding, so assuming that the respondents were correct in their assertion and the High Court was wrong, one must examine the next two hurdles they would have had to surmount.

The Second Hurdle – the Relationship Between International Law and Scots Law

The breach of international law must also be recognised in Scots law. It is not necessarily the case that whatever is part of international law must be part of Scots law also. The relationship between domestic law and international law is controversial. There are essentially two theories at the extremes. One view holds that international law and the laws of all the different states are all part of one coherent system. This is called *monism*. International law is supreme, and because international law defines what a state is, what its territory and jurisdiction are, it also defines the state's capacity to make law, prescribing limits. National law has authority only because international law determines that it should. International law leaves blanks for national law to fill in. National law is a subset of international law. If there is any contradiction between international law and national law, international law overrides it. In such a case national law is not really law at all; it is void.

The other view holds that international law and national law are separate systems. This is called *dualism*. Essentially, both are law, yet their rules may contradict one another, without one law being supreme over the other. This is they are different independent systems. National law does not depend on international law for authority. Thus a national judge may look to a contradiction and say that so far as the domestic legal system is concerned, the domestic legal rule has authority, whereas an international judge would hold that from the

---

[15] Lord Advocate's Reference (No. 1 of 2000) ('LAR'), supra, note 7, paras. [96]–[98].

international perspective the international rule must prevail.

In the United Kingdom a fundamental aspect of the constitution is that Parliament, legally, can make any law it wants to. This includes passing an Act of Parliament that breaches international law. So in *Cheney v. Conn*[16] it was held that the taxpayer had to pay his taxes even if they were being collected for a purpose illegal under international law as an Act of Parliament authorised their collection. This is because Parliament is 'sovereign'. Parliamentary sovereignty is a concept that originated with the English Parliament in 1688 after the 'Glorious Revolution'. Judges up to now have not questioned it a great deal.[17] That is not to say that judges never will. Developments like the entry of the UK into Europe, devolution in Wales and Scotland, and the Human Rights Act 1998 have caused greater interest in the meaning of parliamentary sovereignty. However, it seems likely that parliamentary sovereignty, as a legal rule at least, will be around for a long time yet. Any change would have widespread effects legally and on the political set up of the UK. Related to the concept of parliamentary sovereignty is the rule on treaties. Where the Government agrees to enter a treaty, that treaty has no effect in UK law unless it is given effect by Act of Parliament because it is Parliament and not the Government that makes laws.

This means that for now the United Kingdom is a dualist system, treating international law and national law as separate systems.

The Common Law – Transformation v. Incorporation

Law in Scotland is made up of more than just Acts of Parliament. An important body of law is the common law, or the law made by judges from case to case. As this source of law depends on judges for its development, some judges have indicated that the common law should develop so that it includes all of customary international law. Thus whatever is customary international law is automatically incorporated as

---

[16] [1968] 1 WLR 242, [1968] 1 All ER 779.
[17] For examples of judges questioning the doctrine see Woolf, 'Droit Public – English Style', [1995] *Public Law* 57, at pp. 67–69, Laws 'Law and Democracy' [1995] *Public Law* 72.

part of the common law. This is called the *incorporation* approach. Those who have a conception of law along the monist model are more likely to follow the incorporation approach as it allows them to see domestic common law as limited by international customary law.

Not all judges follow this approach. It is an important rule of our legal system that once a matter has been decided by a superior court, it forms a precedent that must be followed by future courts, including the superior court concerned. Judges follow previous applicable decisions. Because of this some judges refuse to incorporate international law automatically. They will only follow international law if there are no binding court cases on the matter, and only if they think that the rule of international law is a reasonable or just rule. They are free to accept or reject the rule in the same way that they might accept or reject the legal conclusion reached in an English court, an opinion of a legal writer or a principle of ancient Roman law. International law is treated as just a body of principles, like Roman law or English law, which can be drawn upon by Scots judges, but need not be. If there is a previous case on the subject, that will be followed, even if it is based on a now out-of-date rule of international law.[18] The common law is free to contradict international law according to this perspective, as the two systems are separate. This is known as the *transformation* approach.

In short, a breach of international law will only be automatically recognised in Scots law if it is customary law that is being breached and if Scottish judges follow the incorporation approach. This doesn't seem so much of a hurdle, as the law protecting civilians from attack is a rule of customary international law,[19] and the High Court of Justiciary stated 'a rule of customary international law is a rule of Scots law'.[20] However, they may have been wrong. The incorporation approach is not

---

[18] See for example, *Cameron v. HM Advocate* 1971 JC 50, 1971 SLT 202 (piracy in Scots law and international law).

[19] *Advisory Opinion on the Legality of the Threat or Use of Nuclear Weapons* (1996) 35 ILM 809, 1343, at p. 828 of the report, para. [84] of the Opinion, stating that the relevant provisions of the First Additional Protocol to the Geneva Conventions, 1977 (Arts. 48-58), reflected customary international law.

[20] *LAR,* supra, para. [23].

universally followed and there are some theoretical problems with it. For example, if treaties do not form part of Scots law, why should tacit agreements made up of custom have greater effect? Specifically with breaches of international criminal law, the High Court in England & Wales has found problems translating the theoretical criminality of a state in international law into the domestic situation, describing the criminality as 'elusive'.[21] Furthermore, the House of Lords refused to grant permission to extradite General Pinochet to Spain for torture committed in Chile before 1978.[22] Nobody can be extradited to a foreign country for acts that are not crimes in the UK; this is called the 'double criminality' rule. Thus English law required that, as Spain wished to prosecute Pinochet for torture committed abroad, English law must also allow prosecution for torture abroad as well. Although international law granted the UK universal jurisdiction for torture, an Act of Parliament implementing this was only passed in 1978. The House of Lords did not accept that international law could extend the criminal jurisdiction of the English courts before 1978.

The High Court of Justiciary, despite first appearances, seemed to have had problems with international law too. The High Court doubted whether it had the power to consider and pass judgement on the legality of the deployment of the armed forces.[23] This was rather odd. Some exercises of government power[24] can be struck down by courts due to an unreasonable exercise, whilst others are left to the absolute discretion of the Government.[25] This will be because to question how the power was exercised would be to question difficult matters of policy that are not the concern of the courts. However, any purported case of the exercise of

---

[21] *Hutchinson v. DPP,* supra, note 6, *per* Buxton LJ at para. [38].

[22] *R v. Bow Street Metropolitan Stipendiary Magistrate* ex parte *Pinochet Ugarte (No.3)* [2000] 1 AC 147, [1999] 2 WLR 827, [1999] 2 All ER 97.

[23] If a court has the power to examine and pass judgement on an issue, it is *justiciable.* Conversely a matter that is not for the courts to determine is *non-justiciable.*

[24] A 'government power' may be entrusted to ministers by Act of Parliament, or it may exist under the common law. The common law powers of the Government are known collectively as the *royal prerogative.*

[25] See, for example, Lord Roskill's speech in *Council of Civil Service Unions v. Minister for the Civil Service* [1985] AC 374, [1984] 1 WLR 1174, [1984] 3 All ER 935, at p. 418B.

power has to be examined to discover first whether it represents true exercise of legal power with legal effect. Thus the Government's choice to honour certain individuals is something that probably would not be questioned by the courts, even if MBEs and knighthoods were given to people who were racist, or responsible for pollution, or who had been involved with other ethically dubious business. On the other hand, the Government couldn't create honorary MPs in the Commons or confer honorary university degrees, as it is not within its legal power to do so.[26] It may have been that the High Court's unusual reluctance to question the legality of the deployment of the armed forces arose because it would have to apply legal limits from international law that it had never had to consider before. This issue will be revisited further on.[27]

The Third Hurdle – Can Illegality Give Rise to a Defence

Let us assume that my conclusions regarding the second hurdle are wrong. The third hurdle is that the existence of the legal wrong must make available a legal defence to the charge. It is not enough simply that the action was against activity that was legally wrong. 'A person may not take the law into his or her own hands. A person may not commit an offence in an attempt to stop another.'[28] There must be a specific justification or excuse in law for an individual's acts. In Scotland there is no general right to stop crime. There is also no general right in international law to stop international crime. There is a duty (under international law) for those obliged to obey a national law that is a

---

[26] Another example is that the courts will not interfere in the date chosen by the Government to hold a General Election. It is not their place to decide the political matter of whether the election should be held one week or another. However, if HM Government tried to call an election of the Scottish Parliament, this would be interfered with, as the Government does not possess that legal power: Scotland Act 1998, (c. 46), s.3.

[27] For more on the relationship between Scots and international law see my article, 'Conflicting Orders: An examination of the relationship between international law and Scots law', *University of Glasgow Student Law e-Journal,* issue 2:
www.law.gla.ac.uk/Students/Webjourn/V2/JuliusConflict.pdf

[28] *LAR,* para. [36].

breach of international law to nonetheless disobey the national rule.[29] However, the duty not to be complicit in international legal crimes, even if sanctioned by national law, is separate from someone committing positive action to stop an international crime. The accused in the case under discussion also would have fallen at this hurdle. It is at this point that the arguments in the *Lord Advocate's Reference* took a bizarre turn. It had always been maintained that not only was the deployment of Trident a crime but that it was also posing an imminent danger to life. Thus international law and necessity defences had been put forward. As we shall see, the accused resorted to arguing that international law was a relevant defence *by virtue* of necessity.

The Defence of Necessity

As previously mentioned, a person may do what is normally criminal but be justified or excused. Thus a person may deliberately kill someone, but if they were being attacked with a knife in a situation where they had no escape, they would be justified under the defence of self-defence. A person robbing a bank would also normally be committing a crime, but if that person received death threats, he might be excused for what he did by the defence of coercion. This still leaves a number of cases where the accused had no real choice but to do what was normally criminal. Thus a natural disaster such as an earthquake, or a medical emergency such as someone having a heart attack, may call for desperate and normally illegal measures. But these desperate measures are neither covered by self-defence nor coercion. The defence available for situations such as these is that of necessity. It operates as a 'residual excuse'.[30] The High Court quoted a legal writer who noted that necessity 'is in reality a dispensing power exercised by the judges where

---

[29] Second and Fourth 'Nuremberg Principles', see General Assembly Resolutions: 95 (I), (1946); 174 (II), (1947); and 'Formulation of Nürnberg Principles', *Yearbook of International Law Commission,* 1950, vol. 2, 182, at p. 195.

[30] *LAR,* para. [38], quoting *Perka v. The Queen* (1985) 1 DLR (4th) 1 (Canada), *per.* Dickson J. at p. 15.

they are brought to feel that obedience to the law would have endangered some higher value.'[31]

Necessity can appear as a licence to break the law. As such, it is strictly limited by judges. It is a contradiction for a court of law to recognise any higher value than the observance of law. Judges are concerned that necessity may be 'a mask for anarchy'.[32] Indeed, the High Court felt that one lawyer's suggestions as to how the defence of necessity should be broadened would lead to 'anarchy in a particularly shapeless and indeed dangerous form.'[33] It can be seen from this that the judiciary are highly suspicious of the defence of necessity. There was doubt as to whether such a defence existed until the case of *Moss v. Howdle*.[34] There the court held that there was no fundamental difference in a person being coerced to commit a crime because of threats to his life or health, and someone being effectively forced to commit a crime by the threat to his life or health posed by natural disaster or medical emergency. There is one difference, however, as coercion involves someone committing a criminal wrong. Even if the actual coerced perpetrator cannot be punished, his coercer has still committed a crime and is still liable to punishment. This is contrasted with necessity, where an exception to the observance of the law is made without the possibility of finding an alternative person truly responsible. This means no one can be punished for the wrong committed. The practical consequences of this will be examined later.

As an adaptation of the defence of coercion, necessity requires that the circumstances are so terribly dire that the accused has no real choice but to succumb to the threatened catastrophe and break the law. Thus the accused must believe that there is an imminent threat of death or serious injury. His belief must be reasonable. There must be no lawful course of

---

[31] *LAR,* para. [33], quoting Glanville Williams, *Criminal Law: The General Part,* 2nd Edt. (Stevens & Sons, 1961), § 232, p. 728.

[32] *LAR,* para. [52], quoting Lord Justice Edmund-Davies, p. 745H, *Southwark London Borough Council v. Williams* [1971] 1 Ch 734.

[33] *LAR,* para. [52].

[34] 1997 JC 123, 1997 SLT 782, 1997 SCCR 215.

action available. Finally the danger must be such that a reasonable person with the characteristics of the accused would react by breaking the law.

It can be seen then that the definition of necessity is very strictly defined. The Trident Three failed to establish necessity because they were not compelled by the circumstances and were not acting under an imminent danger. The months of meticulous planning and preparation and the calm and deliberate manner in which the sabotage was conducted were entirely inconsistent with the idea that they were acting under a compulsion. In addition, although Trident poses an ever-present danger, that is not the same as stating that the danger is imminent. The possibility of immediate use is insufficient; there must be grounds to believe it *will* occur in the immediate future:

> The actor must have good cause to fear that death or serious injury *would* result unless he acted.[35]

> One might say that there is a chance or possibility that ... [Trident might be used], in some situation that might emerge. But there is no apparent basis for saying that such a situation seemed likely to emerge.[36]

It might be just a matter of time before Trident is used, accidentally, or deliberately, but then it is just a matter of time for all of us. Whilst Trident can be launched at any point with fifteen minutes notice, this is very different from the use of Trident being likely in the next fifteen minutes, or next week, or next year. If it were, the author suspects Trident Ploughshares would have been involved in far more simple and desperate acts to stop Trident, rather than damaging a test barge.

Necessity in Scotland is not, as it is often supposed, a defence to protect the virtuous. It does not exist as a mechanism to allow conduct that the community approves. This is because, as far as the courts are concerned, no breach of the law can be the fit subject of praise. Necessity exists simply to avoid penalising those who had no choice. Punishment

---

[35] *LAR*, para. [42].
[36] *LAR,* para [100].

would serve little value as a deterrent if visited upon those who would have acted as they did anyway (for that is the nature of acting under compulsion). It is more a concession to human behaviour, forgiving its tendencies to be considerate, sympathetic and heroic instead of blindly obedient to the law. This can be seen from the High Court's comments on one suggestion for a formulation of the necessity defence:

> [the formulation is that] the defence is available where the actor believes the conduct to be necessary to avoid an evil, to himself or to another, where ... the evil sought to be avoided by his conduct is greater than that sought to be prevented by the law defining the offence charged ... it appears to suffer from a number of defects for present purposes ... It defines the test in terms of comparative evil without apparent regard to the quality of the conduct threatened. It appears to justify a crime carried out to prevent another crime whenever the threatened crime involved a greater harm.[37]

It is not enough that the accused wished to bring about good in excess of the harm caused.

A residual question is the relevance of the unlawfulness of the danger. Necessity, as has been noted, is a defence derived from the extension of coercion, which concerns criminal threats, to 'threatened' natural disaster or medical emergency. Unlike coercion, there need be no criminal act involved when a volcano erupts, or a person has a heart attack. However, the accused in the *Lord Advocate's Reference* sought to argue that Trident was also illegal under international law. This may have been because the legality of Trident was of far more importance to the respondents than the legality of their acts against it. This was also partly due to the fact that international law was not sufficient in itself to provide a defence; necessity was a vehicle to plug the gaps. The High Court of Justiciary went further than this in the significance it placed on the criminality of the danger. The High Court acknowledged that it was 'not always of the essence'[38] that the

---

[37] *LAR*, para. [55].
[38] *LAR*, para. [19].

danger resulted from criminal acts, insofar as the defence of necessity was concerned. However, the court went on to say:

> ... where the danger arises from some human act or omission, which might be in breach of the criminal law ... the question arises as to what bearing, if any, such considerations might have in judging whether the defence of necessity is established.[39]

The High Court went on to treat the submissions regarding illegality as 'essential' to the necessity defence put forward by the accused. The court found it difficult to see, if 'the Government's actions were thus entirely lawful ... how the defence of necessity could be invoked in relation to the otherwise criminal acts of a third party, done in order to prevent such entirely lawful actions.'[40]

This is a rather difficult part of the *Lord Advocate's Reference*. The problem is that necessity is a *residual* defence relied upon where other defences dependent upon an unlawful element, such as self-defence and coercion, are not available. Classically, illegality is irrelevant to necessity. For example, if a person, without intention or recklessness, creates an imminent danger such as fire or an explosion, he is innocent of any crime. Yet the situation may give rise to a defence of necessity for those who act to avoid the imminent danger. The High Court may in fact have been concerned with a danger created by a *justified* activity. To illustrate what is meant, imagine the following situation. The Death Penalty Act 2003 is passed in Westminster providing that sentence of death by hanging will be imposed upon conviction of an accused person for murder. **B** is convicted of murder and duly sentenced to death. At the point at which **B** is taken to the trap, she has reasonable grounds to fear imminent attack to the danger of her life from **A**, the executioner. She has no means of escape. Ordinarily, **B** would be entitled to use lethal force to protect herself. However, the homicidal attack threatened by **A** is *lawful*, that is to say, it is permitted by law. Thus, that which would

---

[39] *LAR,* para. [35].

normally be murder is justified by law. As such it is not an attack against which self-defence may be used. If **B** killed **A**, she would be guilty of a further act of murder. If anybody came to **B**'s aid and killed **A**, he would also be guilty of murder.

Imagine a slightly different scenario. **B** is still facing execution by **A** except this time **B** seeks to avoid execution by taking **C**, a prison guard, hostage. **C** works in the wings and has no involvement with the executions. Hostage-taking is a crime under statute[41] and is also a serious assault under common law. Self-defence is out of the question as the person assaulted is not the person threatening attack. Coercion is not applicable as **B** is not being threatened by **A** in order to have **C** taken hostage. However, **B** is under an immediate threat of death in circumstances where her will may be overcome, and out of desperation without making any real choice, she takes **C** hostage. She may be acting out of necessity. However, the defence of necessity is not available as the harm threatened is justified by law. It is not illegal, unlike most deliberate killings, which are murder. Thus if the violence threatened is entirely lawful, that is to say justified by law, and a person may not plead self-defence against the perpetrator, then that person certainly cannot plead necessity for causing harm to someone who is completely uninvolved. To return to the Trident, if the attack threatened by Trident was legal by being *justified*, then just as those threatened by the attack could not lawfully resist, or have others resist on their behalf, with all the more reason, those threatened or those acting on their behalf could not cause harm to a person uninvolved in the threatened attack and plead necessity. This exposes two flaws from the judgement of the High Court: (1) an attack on Trident, in its nature homicidal and *prima facie* murder, cannot be justified; (2) direct action against Faslane naval base and associated facilities is not action against an uninvolved third party but against the *very party* threatening the harm.

---

[40] Ibid.
[41] Taking of Hostages Act 1982 (c. 28).

A Dead End?

After dismissing the defences put forward in the *Lord Advocate's Reference* the court stated that there was nothing in 'what the respondents did, or anything in the nature or purposes of the deployment of Trident, [that] indicate any foundation at all, in Scots or in international law, for a defence of justification.'[42] Thus it must be asked whether direct disarmament hit a dead end in the *Lord Advocate's Reference.* The two defences put forward were extremely difficult. The international law defence was based on the assumption that there was nothing in Scots law on the matter. Thus the accused had to establish that the weapons were illegal in terms of a legal system that accepts that innocent civilians may be sacrificed for the wars of the State (albeit provided that such sacrifice would not be unnecessary or disproportionate to the advantage gained).[43] The ruling on whether use of Trident was being 'threatened' was controversial, but the matter only came to that because Trident could not be said to be illegal in the absolute. The burden was upon the accused to argue that a weapon that had a potential lawful use would actually be used in an unlawful manner. The use of international law led to the court being asked to place legal limits on the prerogative that the court would find great difficulty in applying, leading to questions over justiciability. Finally, any illegality was not relevant to whether the accused were guilty: international law did not provide a defence in itself.

This led to the second mistake of the accused. The accused fell back on the defence of necessity to provide themselves with a defence but caused themselves more problems. The High Court held that not only must Trident be illegal, but that:

> ... while such a breach of law is thus a necessary part of the defence of necessity in the circumstances of this case, that fact in no way

---

[42] *LAR,* para. [113].
[43] See the First Additional Protocol to the Geneva Conventions, 1977, supra, note 14.

diminishes the need to establish necessity according to Scots law, taking all appropriate factors into account.[44]

By attempting to make up for the deficiencies of one defence using another they ended up needing to establish both. Necessity was in any case inappropriate as it is a defence for excusing harm to innocent people in times of great peril. It is clear from the emphasis on international law that the accused had more in mind a justification defence targeted against persons responsible for the situation.

Some may argue that the courts' rulings on international law or necessity were wrong or absurd. That is beside the point. The decision is a *precedent* that will be followed in the Sheriff and District Courts, and also in the High Court unless a bench of five judges is convened to review the *Lord Advocate's Reference.* This is unlikely in the extreme.

So it is certainly the end of the road for international law and necessity. But was the High Court right to say that there was no 'foundation at all ... for a defence of justification'? The implicit assumption being made when international law is referred to is that Scots criminal law has nothing to say on the matter. International humanitarian law in its modern form is relatively new. The St. Petersburg Declaration of 1868 set forth grand aspirations to limit the means by which warfare was pursued and to stop unnecessary suffering, but only actually banned a limited class of bullet. The trials at Nuremberg in 1945 did not question the bombing of civilians as targets and the prohibition only became part of treaty law in 1977.[45] In Scotland the first trial regarding conduct towards enemy belligerents was in 1807 when a soldier was sentenced to nine months in prison for killing a prisoner of war.[46] Four years later another soldier was transported for fifteen years, also for killing a prisoner.[47]

---

[44] *LAR,* para. [36].

[45] First Additional Protocol to the Geneva Convention, 1977, supra, Arts. 48–58.

[46] *Ensign Maxwell* (1807), reported in J. Burnett, *A Treatise on Various Branches of the Criminal Law of Scotland* (1811), at p. 77, and W. Buchanan, *Reports of Certain Remarkable Cases in the Court of Session, and Trials in the High Court of Justiciary* (1813), part 2, p. 3.

[47] *Private Inglis* (1811), Burnett, *Criminal Law of Scotland,* at p. 79.

The court noted in both cases that no order could have justified their acts. One hundred and thirty-four years would pass before the Nuremberg Tribunal would hold that superior orders could not excuse.

The author will now examine a potential use of Trident in the context of domestic law. The contention of the author will be that there is a native Scots law of armed conflict and that under this law use of Trident would involve causing unlawful homicide.

Beyond the Lord Advocate's Reference – A New Route

In Scots law a crime is a prohibited combination of facts for which an individual can be held responsible, prosecuted, and punished through a unique procedure. A crime can be usefully separated into two parts. Firstly, there must be some sort of conduct or result that the law prohibits.[48] So, for example, with perjury, someone must state an untruth in court. There must also be an appropriate state of mind so that a person could be held responsible.[49] Thus for perjury, the accused must know that he is not telling the truth.

The Crime of Murder

Murder consists of the destruction of a human life intentionally or with 'wicked recklessness.' Thus the crime of murder operates as a prohibition of a specific result: namely death. It does not matter how you kill someone, whether with fists, or with a knife or with poison. An old and respected criminal wrote:

> ... no distinction seems to be known to the law, with respect to the way in which a person is destroyed. It is equally homicide, whether the deed was done by the hand of the ... [accused], as in shooting or

---

[48] This is known in the criminal law as the *actus reus.*

[49] This is known as the *mens rea,* derived from a Latin phrase: *actus non facit reum nisi mens sit rea,* which roughly translates to: a man may not be guilty because of his acts unless his mind is also guilty. The requirement for *mens rea* is not present in many offences, such as exceeding the speed limit, but it exists for all the crimes discussed in this paper.

stabbing; or by exposing the person to operation of some destructive power, as by confining him to a dungeon without food, or setting fire to the house where he is asleep, or fastening him to a rock in the sea, and leaving him to be drowned there in the flood.[50]

Thus for murder it matters not that the killing is committed with the use of highly sophisticated technological weapons, or with a bow and arrow. Due to its immense power it is impossible to use Trident with any military utility without resulting in people being killed; combatants and non-combatants.

The mental element of murder is that the killing be intentional or that the accused evinces wicked recklessness. Intent is more relevant for our present purposes.[51] For reasons that will be explained later the author concedes that the killing of enemy combatants could be justified under Scots domestic law. However, it is impossible to conceive of any military use of Trident that would not kill non-combatants. It may be that within the nuclear submarine crews there are idiots, or those who seek to deny or avoid the obvious; namely that their acts would lead to inevitable civilian loss of life. However, under Scots law the mental element of a crime is inferred from the facts.[52] Thus it can be inferred from the use of a 100Kt nuclear warhead that civilian loss of life was foreseen and accepted, and thus intended, because a reasonable person would have foreseen it. If the crews who fired the weapon, or the superiors who ordered them, were in error as to the effects, that error would only excuse if it were reasonable.[53]

---

[50] David Hume, *Commentaries on the Law of Scotland Respecting Crimes*, 4th edition (1844), at p. 189. Hume's *Commentaries* are of great authority on the common law, as they were written during a period when there was little academic reporting of court cases. David Hume was the nephew of his namesake philosopher, who was also a lawyer.

[51] Whether someone's conduct can be characterised as reckless depends on the risks involved and the care that could have been taken. Thus someone's conduct, though risky, may not be reckless due to the circumstances (e.g. wartime).

[52] For example, where **A** throws a punch at **B** it can be inferred that **A** intended to assault **B**. Equally, should **A** head-butt **B**, assault could be inferred except where the circumstances suggest otherwise, such as if **A** and **B** were playing football and **A** was trying to make contact with a crossed ball.

[53] This is because the mental element in Scotland is assessed objectively according to the standards of the reasonable person: e.g. *Dewar v. HM Advocate* 1945 JC 5, 1945 SLT 114,

In the context of this case it is clear such a mistake could not be reasonably held.

On the face of it, any use of Trident would constitute the crime of murder. This is only true, however, if the result cannot be justified under the criminal law.

Justifications

A justification is a set of circumstances that means that what would normally be criminal is in fact permitted and sanctioned by the law. It is a type of defence to a crime. In relation to Trident there are a number of defences that may be relevant. These defences will be discussed in turn to examine whether any could justify the use of Trident.

Self-Defence

Self-defence is the right of a person to use physical violence to stop an unlawful attack against him. It could be argued that Trident might be used to stop an imminent enemy threat of the use of a weapon of mass destruction. However, self-defence in Scots law differs from self-defence in the international legal sense in that this defence is concerned with whether the individuals harmed are responsible for an unlawful attack, as opposed to the responsibility of the state that they are situated in. 'Domestic' self-defence is more difficult to establish. Self-defence could only justify the harm against those involved in such an attack and not ordinary non-combatants. It would not be available.

Necessity

As has been discussed above, the defence of necessity is to prevent the injustice of someone being punished for something that he was compelled to do by circumstances. It is an excuse and not a justification.

---

relating to error in theft. *Jamieson v. HM Advocate* 1994 SLT 537, 1994 SCCR 181, concerning rape, has cast doubt on this, but the great weight of authority still suggests the objective approach.

This differs from the international legal definition of 'military necessity' which is the allowance given to states when they have lawfully decided to use armed force against another state.[54] Although someone pleading necessity could be acquitted, this does not alter the fact that an unlawful attack took place against which action could be taken. The defence could probably not be established in any case, as it is doubtful whether necessity is a defence to murder.[55]

Superior Orders

Superior orders is a defence under Scots law for members of the armed forces to show that they were following an order of the superior, or were acting in pursuance of their general military duty. However, orders that are 'flagrantly and violently wrong'[56] must not be followed. This qualification shows that superior orders is simply a concession to military discipline and is an excuse only. Much for the same reason as with necessity, an accused successfully pleading superior orders would not alter the fact that an unlawful attack had taken place.

Royal Prerogative and Act of State

The royal prerogative is the collective term for the powers exercised by the Government under the common law. A prerogative power is capable of making lawful what would otherwise be unlawful. Relevant for our purposes are the prerogatives of declaring war, of deployment of the armed forces and of the defence of the realm. The related issue of acts of state will also be considered.

The Prerogative of Declaring War

The matter of war used to be quite formalistic; there was an exact point, in

---

[54] Action is lawful where in 'self-defence' of the state or other states (Charter of the United Nations, 1945, Art. 51), or when authorised by the UN Security Council.

[55] It is not a defence to murder in England: *R v. Dudley* (1884) 14 QBD 273.

[56] *HM Advocate v. Hawton*, (1861) 4 Irv 58 *per* Lord Justice-General M'Neill, at p. 72.

legal terms, when it could be ascertained whether the country was at peace or at war. In domestic law the matter of whether the country was at war with an enemy was determined solely by the opinion of HM Government which could not be questioned on this point. Under domestic law the UK was still at war with Germany until 1951 even though the country had been invaded, had unconditionally surrendered and was under the occupation of the allied powers. In terms of international law Germany did not exist, but the UK was still at war with it because the Foreign Secretary said so.[57] The opinion of the Government that a war has commenced is expressed in the form of a 'declaration of war'. The question is: what effect does that declaration have?

Those who are not British citizens but who reside in the UK can be described as 'friendly aliens'. The effect of a declaration of war is firstly to change the status of the citizens of the country the UK is at war with, from 'friendly alien' to 'enemy alien'. It also makes contracts with those engaged in business in enemy territory unenforceable. The Government has the legal power in common law to detain or expel all enemy aliens within the UK. They can be treated as prisoners of war. However, they do retain the ability to enter contracts, to marry, to be prosecuted or sued and to sue others.[58] They cannot raise a legal action to question their captivity as the Government may lawfully detain them under the prerogative. However, the Government is itself subject to limits in the manner in which it deals with enemy aliens. Any restrictions on aliens, or even captivity of aliens, are signs that they are being permitted to stay in the UK.[59] Thus they remain here with the permission of the Crown and are subject to the protection of the Crown's courts. In the Scots cases of *Ensign Maxwell* (1807)[60] and *Private Inglis* (1810),[61] concerning the deaths of prisoners of war, it was noted that a soldier need not follow every order from his superiors; he must disobey those orders that were

---

[57] *R v. Bottrill* ex parte *Kuechenmeister* [1947] KB 41, [1946] 2 All ER 434.
[58] McNair & Watts, *Legal Effects of War in English Law,* 4th Edt., (Cambridge University Press, 1966), at p. 93.
[59] *Schaffenius v. Goldberg* [1916] 1 KB 284.
[60] Supra, note 44.

manifestly illegal. This suggests that prisoners of war were under protection from private citizens and also that the Government was limited in what orders it could issue concerning prisoners of war. Thus enemy prisoners had legal rights of protection enforceable against the Government. Subjects of enemy countries were still entitled to legal protections: harm to them had to be justified under specific legal powers. However, the reader might notice that only those who are in the UK with the permission of the Crown, such permission evidenced by captivity or other restrictions upon enemy aliens, are dealt with. It does not deal with a combatant who has not been caught, or a spy who is secretly living in the country.

The question in these circumstances is the significance of detention or restriction. Does detention or other restrictions on aliens (such restrictions conferring upon the aliens rights of protection from the Crown) bring about a grant of substantive rights by the Crown? Alternatively, does detention simply allow the captive to enforce rights that already existed before his capture.

It appears that foreign nationals can pursue legal actions to enforce rights that accrued to them during the war whilst they were enemy aliens. This is the case despite the fact that, at the time, they were under absolutely no protection from the Crown and could not enforce those rights whilst the war continued.[62] This shows that captivity merely allows enforcement of rights that already exist; thus enemy aliens can still be the subjects of unlawful attack. Were this not so, enemy aliens could not be the subjects of criminal prosecution for acts before capture, such as war crimes, as they would neither be the subject of legal rights nor liabilities in terms of the captor's law.

Perhaps the final point to make in this context is that declarations of war are unheard of now. Although armed forces have been deployed in

---

[61] Supra, note 45.

[62] See *The Berwickshire* [1950] 205; *Hugh Stevenson and Sons Ltd. v. Aktiengesellschaft für Carton-Nagen-Industrie* [1918] AC 239. Lord Atkinson in *Hugh Stevenson* noted that it is a mistake if 'the temporary suspension of the remedy is confounded with the 'permanent loss of the right', at p. 253. See also McNair & Watts, supra, pp. 327–329.

Afghanistan, Argentina, Egypt, Iraq, Korea and Serbia, the last war that the UK was involved in, as far as the law is concerned, was the Second World War.

The Prerogative of the Deployment of the Armed Forces

The question is whether use of Trident and its effects would fall within the lawful limits of the prerogative of the deployment of armed forces. If it falls outwith those limits, it cannot form the basis of a justification of what would normally be a criminal act.

In *China Navigation Co. v. Attorney-General*[63] the plaintiffs sought to challenge the decision of the Government to charge for the service of armed forces to preserve security. The plaintiffs argued that although the Government was entitled to make an assessment as to what deserved protection, once they had made that assessment, they were bound to provide protection to whatever in their judgement needed it. They could not make a charge for what they were bound to provide. The court held that the decision on whether or not to deploy armed forces was a prerogative power that could not be questioned by a court; thus it was solely for the Government's discretion to provide armed forces and to charge for the service.

In *Chandler v. DPP*[64] the accused were anti-nuclear protesters charged with offences under official secrets legislation. The offence required the conduct to be 'prejudicial to the safety or interests of the state'. The accused sought to argue that action against nuclear weapons was conducive to the safety and interests of the State. On appeal to the House of Lords it was held that the question of whether nuclear arms were conducive to the safety or in the interests of the state was to be decided by the Government, as its decision on the deployment of the armed forces, as discussed in the *China Navigation* case, was within the prerogative. It can be seen that matters of national security and armed forces policy were for the Government, so that it could not be argued

---

[63] [1932] 2 KB 197.

that their judgement over security prejudiced the state's safety or that the armed forces policy was not in the state's interests. That would lead to questioning the merits of the Government's policy decision.

In the *Lord Advocate's Reference* the prerogative of the deployment of the armed forces was mentioned with the High Court suggesting that the issue might not be justiciable.[65] When courts examine the exercise of a legal power they can do so on three grounds. The first ground is illegality, where the person has purported to do something under a power that in fact exceeds the limits of that power. These limits might be expressed in a statute that creates the power, the common-law limits of a prerogative power and the limits imposed by other statutes (most importantly now the Scotland Act 1998 and the Human Rights Act 1998). An example, as mentioned earlier, would be a minister recommending to the sovereign an appointment of an honorary MP, purportedly under the prerogative of honour. The second ground is that the exercise would be procedurally improper, because the procedural requirements of notice to affected parties, hearings, etc., had not been complied with. Alternatively, a common law requirement of natural justice may be an example of procedural impropriety. Finally, the exercise of a power may be challenged because it is inexplicable or irrational, perhaps with no support from evidence, so that no reasonable decision-maker could have exercised the power in that way.[66]

The reader may notice that the word 'illegal' can be used in a broad sense to mean that it is something that a court of law will stop, or in a narrow sense to mean that it is something that a court of law will stop specifically because it is not a real exercise of a power at all as it exceeds the limits of that power.[67]

It has been asserted time and again that the prerogative can be reviewed on grounds of illegality. However, in some circumstances the

---

[64] [1964] AC 763.

[65] *LAR*, at paras. [56-60], [73].

[66] *Council of Civil Service Unions v. Minister for the Civil Service* [1985] AC 374, [1984] 1 WLR 1174, [1984] 3 All ER 935, *per* Lord Diplock at pp. 410D–411B.

subject matter of the prerogative is not such as to imply any real procedural requirements, or to allow review on the grounds that the exercise of power was irrational or unreasonable. Examples of relevance are the deployment of armed forces and national security. In the *GCHQ*[68] case decided in the House of Lords, Lord Diplock noted that matters of national security were prime examples of matters to be left to the Government. Interestingly, we went on to state:

> ... that a decision of which the ultimate source of power to make it is not a statute but the common law (whether or not the common law is ... given the label 'the prerogative') may be the subject of judicial review on the ground of illegality is, I think, established by the cases cited by ... [a fellow judge in that case], and this extends to cases where the field of law to which this decision relates is national security, as the decision of this House itself in *Burmah Oil Co. Ltd. v. Lord Advocate*[69] shows.[70]

Clearly, review on grounds of illegality must be available in all cases. If it were not, how could it be determined that a decision would be a legally effective use of power in the first place and not to be interfered with? How can you tell that a prerogative has been used without looking at the nature of the prerogative invoked and its extent?

From this it can be seen that *Chandler* could only have been concerned with the merits or wisdom of the Government's decision to deploy nuclear weapons; no one in that case questioned whether the decision might be illegal by being beyond the limits of the Government's legal power. Review *was* available for the prerogatives of deployment and the defence of the realm. The High Court in the *Lord*

---

[67] Clyde & Edwards, *Judicial Review,* (W. Green, 2002), deal with this matter at paras. 15.01 and 15.02.

[68] *Council of Civil Service Unions v. Minister for the Civil Service* [1985] AC 374, [1984] 1 WLR 1174, [1984] 3 All ER 935.

[69] 1964 SC (HL) 117. It was held by the House of Lords in that case that the Government must pay compensation when it uses its prerogative power to confiscate or destroy property during wartime.

[70] *CCSU v. Minister for the Civil Service*, supra, note 68, at p. 411C.

Advocate's Reference suggested otherwise, but it must be noted that they appeared to have confused the narrow and broad senses of illegality: they refer to one case as concerning legality when the ground of review sought was that the policy was unreasonable or irrational.[71] Opinions suggesting exercises of the prerogative could not be reviewed referred to the grounds of review in general and not illegality specifically; indeed the question of illegality must be addressed first to determine whether what is being dealt with is a true exercise of a prerogative.

Now it is appropriate to ask: is it within the legal limits of the prerogative of deployment to deploy armed forces in a manner that constitutes a criminal offence? The answer must be 'no' or otherwise a general immunity from criminal law would be conferred upon soldiers by the commands of the Government and it has already been noted that soldiers cannot be excused for following manifestly unlawful orders.

National Security

It is within the prerogative of the Government to decide what is necessary for the defence of the realm. This is often called 'national security'. The judgement of the Government cannot be called into question. However, this does not mean that the Government has a universal power to act in the interests of the state. The ancient English case of *Entick v. Carrington*[72] is authority that there is no general power to act out of state necessity. Considerations of state necessity are relevant only in connection with specific legal powers. If the Government therefore exercises its legal power to deport an individual, or to vary the working conditions of those in the civil service, national security considerations might be a factor in how those powers are exercised. Someone being deported may not be told the specific

---

[71] *LAR* at para. [59], referring to *R v. Ministry of Defence* ex parte *Smith* [1996] QB 517, [1996] 2 WLR 305. [1996] 1 All ER 257.
[72] (1765) 19 State Tr 1029.

evidence behind the Home Secretary's decision to deport him,[73] or civil service workers may not be consulted in advance about changes to working conditions.[74] Provided the Government believes national security requires it, that decision will not be questioned. But this privilege of unquestioned judgement relates only to the judgement alone, and any action in defence of the realm must also be capable of separate legal justification. A decision that the defence of the realm required the use of Trident could not be questioned, but the legality of the consequences of such use could.

Act of State Doctrine

Acts of state can be described as actions on behalf of the Crown that are not to be questioned in the courts. Act of state in this sense could mean acts under the prerogative that should not be interfered with by the courts, and it is in this sense that some courts have used the term. However, that does not give details about what acts of the Government must be recognised and respected, and it confuses the prerogative with a different doctrine: that concerning justiciability.[75]

In this sense, an act of state is an act commanded or ratified by the Crown that harms someone who is not a British subject and is outwith the realm.[76] This is because the victim of an act of state does not owe allegiance to the sovereign and the sovereign does not owe the victim a reciprocal duty of protection. This goes as far as preventing those beyond the Crown's protection from questioning the actions of the Crown in the Crown's courts. Thus it could be argued that Trident could not be considered to be unlawful as the victims, being foreigners abroad, would have no entitlement to claim compensation for an unlawful act

---

[73] *R v. Secretary of State* ex parte *Hosenball* [1977] 1 WLR 766, [1977] 3 All ER 452. The law on expulsion of immigrants for the purposes of national security has been amended by statute, but the general principle holds true.

[74] *CCSU v. Minister for the Civil Service*, supra, note 68, at p. 411C.

[75] The definition of act of state used by Lord Reid in *Attorney-General* v. *Nissan* [1970] AC 179 is being used.

[76] Act of state also probably applies to enemy aliens within the realm.

against them.

However, the fact that the act concerned can be classified as an act of state does not mean that the harm caused is justified. *Johnstone v. Pedlar*[77] dealt with the question of whether act of state could be pleaded against a friendly alien. Lord Atkinson noted:

> It is in the authorities quite clear that the injury afflicted upon an individual by the act of state of a sovereign authority does not by reason of the nature of the act by which the injury is inflicted cease to be a wrong. What these authorities do establish is that a remedy for the wrong cannot be sought for in the Court of the sovereign authority ...

An attack by Trident may not be something for which foreigners abroad could sue but it would not cease to be a wrong. It would be necessary for the court to take cognisance of the wrongful act in assessing whether the acts of an accused were criminal; to do otherwise would have the effect of pleading act of state against those who are in the allegiance of the Crown. The difference between justification and lack of remedy is illustrated by the situation of ambassadors. Ambassadors cannot be prosecuted for crimes or sued in civil courts,[78] but that does not mean their acts are justified. An individual is entitled to come to the aid of someone attacked by an ambassador.

Soldier's Defence

Little reference to international law has so far been made. In the first part of this submission it was argued that international law was not a formal source of Scots law, but it was also noted that it could be drawn upon as a body of legal doctrine. To this point the research has demolished various defences and it seems nothing under Scots law would justify any acts of war. This would be absurd, if not undesirable.

---

[77] [1921] 2 AC 262.
[78] This is called 'diplomatic immunity' and is intended to stop Governments putting pressure on a foreign state's representatives through legal action.

It is thus appropriate to ask, when there do not appear to be any common law cases on the subject, if it would be appropriate to draw upon international law. To answer this, the nature of criminal liability of individuals under international law needs to be examined.

International Criminal Liability

The traditional sources of international law are treaty, custom and general principles of law, with legal writings and cases being an aid to interpreting the law. This is in line with positivist international legal thought that sees legal obligation as something consented to by states, by entering a treaty or continuing (or not objecting to) a custom. It is difficult to see how this can have much application to individuals, who cannot enter international obligations to obey certain laws.

International criminal law can be seen in three different contexts. Firstly, international criminal law could be seen as giving rights to states to exercise jurisdiction over those who are not their nationals for war crimes etc., committed against it, without complaint from the state to which the accused persons belong. Secondly, international criminal law could be seen as creating obligations upon states to prosecute those guilty of crimes such as war crimes towards the state whose nationals were victims (e.g. as the USA claimed from the former Afghanistan government regarding the Twin Towers attacks). Obligations may also be owed to the international community of states where a heinous crime such as torture is concerned. Finally, international criminal law could be seen as generating general principles derived from treaties and custom which states agree should apply to how they deal with such as alleged war criminals.

It is the contention of this work that there is no comprehensive system or code of criminal law, derived either from custom or treaty, and that international law concerns itself primarily with matters of jurisdiction and obligations of enforcement.

This can be most easily demonstrated if one looks to the closest step so far to a comprehensive criminal code: the International

Criminal Court Treaty.[79] Two examples will suffice. Article 6 defines genocide as, among other things, killing members of any national, ethnic, racial or religious group with intent to destroy that group. Article 7 prohibits crimes against humanity, which include murder, torture and rape, but only where they are part of a widespread or systematic attack against civilians. It does not follow that murder, torture or rape committed out of individual enmity is lawful as such under international law, or that a state would be precluded from prosecuting a foreign soldier for murder committed upon its soil. This enigma is best made sense of if the ICC Treaty is seen as an agreement by the contracting States as to what crimes they will allow to be prosecuted before an international court, whether or not they consent, and whether or not the criminal allegation involves its nationals or territory. The treaty is consent to jurisdiction. It can further be seen as an expression of the obligation upon states to prosecute crimes of such serious gravity that any state should prosecute them, regardless of whether the individual criminal allegation has any connection whatsoever to the state concerned.[80]

The Nuremberg Trial[81] appeared to hold that the law being applied directly upon the accused was that of international law. This is not the same as international law conferring the right and/or obligation upon the individual states to punish the accused. It must be said that this ruling was unnecessary as the Tribunal's Charter prohibited it from questioning the validity of the 'international law' set out in it, and that it was the intention of the states party to the Charter that the legality of the Tribunal's proceedings should not be called into question. The ruling on international law also contradicts the statement by the Tribunal that its establishment was a special exercise of each state party to the Tribunal's

---

[79] Rome Statute of the International Criminal Court, 2002.

[80] It is important to note in this respect that the crimes of genocide and torture are crimes of universal jurisdiction with States under treaty obligations to punish all offenders. It is also significant to note the article on subject jurisdiction, Art. 5: 'The jurisdiction of the Court shall be limited to the most serious crimes of concern to the international community as a whole'.

[81] International Military Tribunal for the Trial of the Major German War Criminals.

Charter.[82] To make sense of the Nuremberg Tribunal's continued affirmation of direct responsibility, this must be seen as an expression that states, whether by establishing their own courts or collaborating with others, have the right and/or duty to punish individuals for certain specific acts.[83]

This being so, it would be inappropriate to transform the rules of international criminal law into municipal law. It would be impossible to construct a defence to a charge of murder on the basis that the acts complained of were in pursuance of armed conflict and not illegal under international law. The lack of illegality simply demonstrates a lack of jurisdiction or obligation to try and punish. International criminal law could not be seen as conferring an immunity on all acts undertaken by command of a state that did not violate international criminal law, as international crimes may be prosecuted after any length of time according to international law[84] (even if an individual state may normally put a limit on prosecutions of, say, twenty years) and often states possess extra-territorial jurisdiction and even sometimes a duty to prosecute. This is inconsistent with the idea that with some acts it is appropriate to test their legality according to municipal criminal law and with other acts it is appropriate to test their legality according to

---

[82] *Trial of German Major War Criminals [Proceedings of the Nuremberg Tribunal]*, (HMSO, 1950), part 22, pp. 443–4, Judgement of the Tribunal:

> The making of the Charter was the exercise of the sovereign legislative power by the countries to which the German Reich surrendered, … [it is] the undoubted right of these countries to legislate for the occupied territories.
>
> The signatory Powers created this Tribunal … In doing so, they have done together what any one of them might have done singly.

Also the Moscow Declaration, 1943, made by the UK, USA and USSR, refers to bringing German war criminals back to the territories of their crimes for trial, and only refers to trial by international tribunal of those criminals whose crimes have no specific geographical location.

[83] See G. Schwarzenberger, *International Law, as applied by international courts and tribunals*, Vol. 2, *Law of Armed Conflict*, (Stevens & Co., 1968), especially at p. 519 where he argues that international criminal jurisdiction should be seen as a form of extraordinary State jurisdiction justified under the principles of reprisal, rather than as a body of substantive law.

[84] Convention on the Non-Applicability of Statutory Limitations to Crimes Against Humanity and War Crimes, 1968. The United Kingdom is not a party to this convention.

international law. If it were simply a matter of applying the proper law, there would be no reason to have such strong powers of prosecution. To state otherwise would be an inversion of the history of international criminal law: that of municipal law contributing to international law and not the other war around.[85] The manner in which municipal legislation is enacted supports this.[86] It is perhaps appropriate to remind ourselves that the trials in Scotland for crimes against prisoners of war took place in 1807 and 1811. International criminal law simply provides for the better prosecution of certain acts of particular concern to the community of states on account of their severity or their international context.

If this were not the case then it would follow that all crimes with an international context must be tried according to what substantive international criminal law exists at the point of the date of alleged commission. If this is so, it follows that there is a strong argument that the accused at Nuremberg should have been acquitted of many of the charges against them, as it was far from clear that there did exist international crimes of aggression and crimes against humanity, even though what the accused did was clearly murderous.

---

[85] Schwarzenberger, supra, p. 15 states that the origin of international criminal law lies in municipal legislation passed to regulate states' own armed forces, such legislation upon which being accepted by other states constituting a general usage that eventually gains the force of law.

[86] For example, Australia: War Crimes Act 1945 as amended by the War Crimes Amendment Act 1988, provides that 'serious crimes' such as murder may be prosecuted in Australia where they were committed in pursuance of the Second World War and committed in Europe. Thus the Act operates to extend jurisdiction of the Australian courts. It is a defence to a charge that the acts did not constitute a crime under international law. (See G. Triggs, 'All Pity Choked, Australia's War Crimes Trials', McCormack & Simpson (Eds.), *The Law of War Crimes: National and International Approaches* (Kluwer, 1997), p. 123, at pp. 127–9.) The Criminal Code of Canada, s. 7, provides that the Canadian courts will have jurisdiction to prosecute acts criminal by the law of Canada and of international law, wherever they occur. In a bizarre ruling, the Supreme Court of Canada ruled by a 4-3 majority that the provision required the requisite mental awareness, not only of the Canadian crime, but of the 'inhumanity' of the international crime as the provision did not simply extend jurisdiction (*R v. Finta* (1994) CR (4th) 265). S. Williams argues this is wrong, see 'Laudable Principles Lacking Application: Prosecution of War Criminals in Canada', McCormick & Simpson, *Law of War Crimes*, p. 151, at pp. 159, 166–167. In the UK the War Crimes Act 1991 (c. 13), s. 1(1) provides that 'proceedings for murder, manslaughter or culpable homicide may be brought' where they occurred in German-held territories during the Second World War and constituted a breach of the law of war.

Scots Law on Armed Conflict

If international law should not be imported into Scots law does that mean that all armed conflict is illegal? Well, unfortunately not. There is an old defence best described as soldier's duty or privilege.[87] The privilege consists of the right of soldiers to defend themselves. As will be explained later, the usual requirements for self-defence would be that the danger was imminent, that there was no opportunity to escape and that the force was proportionate. However, in the context of riots it has been said that soldiers may pursue their duty and need not escape, and use force to remain at their post if necessary. They may also use force, including lethal force, where necessary to keep their weapons, to prevent themselves being surprised and to keep themselves in fit bodily condition to defend themselves. To put it simply, they could use force to pursue their lawful duty and to protect themselves whilst doing their duty. It should also be noted that in the past judicial officers executing criminal warrants were permitted to use force in self defence and pursue their duty in the face of opposition rather than retreat. This could have application to armed combat against enemy belligerents. It should be recalled that two of the prerogative powers of the Crown are the defence of the realm and the deployment of armed forces. The author concluded earlier that the power to deploy the armed forces consisted of the right to make unchallengeable policy decisions regarding the appropriate occasions and manner in which armed forces could be deployed and that actual justification was still required in the context of another power. It perhaps may be safely stated that the defence of the realm is a lawful purpose for which armed forces may be deployed. Thus it would be a lawful duty of soldiers to defend the realm, to repel invasions or air raids and other attacks against the United Kingdom. They would not need to wait for an imminent danger but could use force against any danger that posed a threat to the soldiers carrying out their duty (to

---

[87] The cases involve members of the Army or Militias but the principle is applicable to all combatants in the service of the Crown.

defend the realm) and any threat that could surprise them in their duty. This could give considerable scope for pre-emptive action (such as air-strikes) against enemies. It is also interesting in this context that it lies within the prerogative for the Crown to annex territory.[88] Thus it would be a lawful duty of soldiers, if ordered, to seek to establish control over foreign territory, and if resisted in this duty, they could use lethal force. They would be entitled to pursue their duty in the face of opposition and use force to defend themselves. In essence, the defence of soldiers' (or combatants') duty would be wide enough to include all acts targeted against (openly or secretly) hostile enemies, whether it meant repelling an invasion or invading enemy territory. Soldiers would be protected from criminal liability for acts targeted against hostile enemies but killing civilians where there was no intent to kill civilians. If there was no intent to attack a civilian then the only crime in question could be culpable homicide. Culpable homicide requires an objective standard of recklessness and thus the combatant's acts would be compared to how other combatants would have acted in that situation. Only if a combatant's acts fell well below the standard of care to be expected of a combatant whilst in armed conflict would he be held guilty, and it may be that juries would not expect too high a standard of care in the 'fog of war'.

However, cases involving soldiers' duty only involve those situations where the accused acted against those who were resisting the soldier in his duty – it can have no application to those who have not sought to resist the soldier. Any attack that will knowingly and inevitably cause the deaths of those who are not resisting, i.e. non-combatants, must be regarded as an intentional destruction of life, and as such, murder.

Relevance of Unlawfulness of an Attack by Trident

If it is true to say that any use of Trident would involve the crime of murder under Scots law and be an unlawful homicide, then the next

---

[88] *Post Office v. Estuary Radio* [1968] 2 QB 740, [1967] 3 All ER 663, [1967] 1 WLR 1396.

question that must arise is whether it makes a jot of difference to the fate of the direct activist before the courts. It was noted earlier that there is no right in Scots or international law to commit a crime to prevent a crime. However, the relevance of examining whether any use of Trident would appear to be a crime, and then to examine whether there was any legal justification available, was to demonstrate that use of Trident would involve the use of unlawful violence. It would be an unlawful attack. The defence of self-defence in Scots law is available to prevent or stop unlawful attacks.[89] The attack may be targeted against the accused, or someone whom the accused was seeking to help.[90] The questions to be answered concerning such a defence are: (a) whether self-defence is an appropriate plea to a defence such as breach of the peace by blockade or malicious damage by fence-cutting or other sabotage; (b) what the requirements of self-defence are in these circumstances; and, (c) whether direct action against Trident comes within the requirements of self-defence.

Appropriateness of Self-Defence Plea

Self-defence is a defence pleaded against charges of murder, culpable homicide and assault. Typical Trident Ploughshares actions lead to charges of malicious damage and breach of the peace. Is self-defence available as a defence to non-violent crimes?

Butcher v. Jessop[19] involved an Old Firm match in which fighting between the players resulted. It seems that the police had been concerned about the effect this might have on the audience, possibly leading to a riot, rather than about the players themselves. They were charged with breach of the peace: not assault. It was nonetheless held by the High Court that self-defence was available to an assault-type breach of the peace. However, the question is whether it would be available to

---

[89] *HM Advocate v. Carson* 1964 SLT 21 *per* Lord Wheatley at p. 21: 'If a man sees another man being attacked, he is entitled to try and stop that unlawful attack.'
[90] *HM Advocate v. Carson,* supra.; *Fitzpatrick v. HM Advocate* 1992 SLT 796.
[91] 1989 SLT 593, 1989 JC 55, 1989 SCCR 119.

justify non-violent acts. In the absence of self-defence, necessity would need to be pleaded to justify those acts. As has been pointed out, necessity is strictly defined by judges who hold it in suspicion. The person's will must be overborne, whereas with self-defence force against non-life threatening attacks is permissible. It seems likely that necessity would not be a defence to murder.[92] Thus necessity is a stricter test to meet.

The rationale of self-defence suggests that it must be available as a plea to all crimes where the target of defensive action is responsible as an aggressor behind an unlawful attack. Contrast the two following situations. **A** threatens **B** with a catapult; this is an unlawful attack. If **B** uses force to disarm **A**, this may be justified by self-defence. Alternatively, if **B** instead utters coarse threats, telling **A** to f* off, does it follow that to avoid a conviction for breach of the peace, **B**'s acts must meet the stricter test of necessity?

A similar question must be asked with malicious damage. **A** again threatens **B** with a catapult. **B,** in the course of disarming **A**, breaks the catapult to make sure **A** can't use it against him. Must the attack on **A** be examined according to the more indulgent standards of self-defence whilst the damage to his weapon must meet stricter standards? Is the person who prefers non-injurious courses of action to personal violence to be penalised? Is a person's property to be protected better than their person?

Whilst the matter has never come before the courts it is submitted that the court would apply the test of who was (potentially) harmed by the acts in question and see if this was the same as the person who was an unlawful aggressor towards the accused. Thus in *Tudhope v. Grubb*[93] where a drunk man drove off in a car to avoid his assailants, it was clear that the acts had to be tested according to the necessity standard, as the potential victims were other road users and pedestrians, even though the harm avoided was one typical to a plea of self-defence.[94]

---

[92] *R v. Dudley* (1884) 14 QBD 273 – no defence in English law.
[93] 1983 SCCR 351.
[94] See comments by G. H. Gordon, 1983 SCCR, at p. 352.

The Requirements of Self-Defence

The usual requirements of self-defence are that there be (a) an imminent danger of (b) unlawful attack where (c) there are no reasonable means of escape, and that the force used was (d) proportionate to the attack threatened and not cruelly excessive and (e) was not more than was necessary. It has been noted earlier that the requirement for imminent danger poses a problem for those engaged in direct action against an enduring danger.

It was noted in the case of *HM Advocate v. Doherty* that where escape is possible, escape 'is really just another way of ridding yourself of the danger ... [An accused] could escape or retreat, and then no necessity arises to retaliate by the use of a lethal weapon or in any other way ... '.[95] It could be argued that the requirements of self-defence are primarily that it is necessary and proportionate, and that this can be broken down into further requirements: that it is necessary where there is an imminent danger, and thus no time for alternative means to avoid the attack, such as contacting the police or escaping, as force would also be unnecessary in that context as well. Furthermore, no more force than necessary may be used.[96]

The case of *Thomson v. HM Advocate*[97] supports this view. In this case the accused argued that he had been coerced into committing a bank robbery by threats made against his family. The trial judge had directed that only threats of *immediate* harm could form the basis of a defence of coercion. The accused appealed. The High Court looked to an old writer on the matter, who had said that:

> ... generally, and with relation to the ordinary condition of a well-regulated society, where every man is under the shield of law, and has the means of resorting to that protection, this is at least a difficult plea ... for any atrocious crime, unless ... [there is] an immediate danger of

---

[95] *HM Advocate* v. *Doherty* 1954 JC 1 at p. 5.
[96] See e.g. *Pollock v. HM Advocate* 1998 SLT 880.
[97] *Thomson v. HM Advocate* 1983 SCCR 368, 1983 JC 69, 1983 SLT 682.

death or great bodily harm ...[98]

The High Court recognised that the requirement for imminent danger was prefaced with 'generally', and that:

> ... even in the ordinary condition of a well-regulated society there may be circumstances where a person is exposed to a threat of violence to himself or a third party or even the security of the state from which he cannot be protected from the forces of law.[99]

The High Court declined to state what would be the situation in such a case but it seems likely that such a requirement would not be insisted upon. A commentator to the case notes:

> ... the parallels with self-defence are obvious: the crime is excused only where it was 'necessary' for the accused to commit it in order to avoid the threatened danger; and the danger must therefore be imminent, since *otherwise* it could be avoided by recourse to the protection of the authorities in the interim.[100]

The question must arise whether imminent danger would remain a requirement for self-defence where there can be no effective recourse to the authorities, since in that case force remains necessary. If imminent danger would not be required for coercion (an excuse) in such circumstances, then with all the greater force of reason, imminent danger should not be required for self-defence, (a justification). It should be noted at this point that in the author's opinion imminent danger would still be required of necessity as an indication that the will of the accused was overborne. The reasons there might be stricter limits to necessity than to coercion would be that with coercion an illegal situation is still recognised for which someone can be punished.

---

[98] Hume, *Commentaries on the Law of Scotland Respecting Crimes*, 4th Edt., (1844), Vol. 1, p. 53.
[99] *Per* Lord Justice-Clerk Wheatley, delivering the opinion of the court, at p. 381.
[100] G. H. Gordon, 1983 SCCR, at p. 383.

Coercion shifts culpability whilst necessity extinguishes it.

Is there available effective recourse to the authorities? Let us assume the author was to take his claim that Trident was illegal to the courts. The objections that would be made would be that as an ordinary individual the author had no legal interest in the question of the legality of an attack by Trident.[101] Furthermore, the only people who would have an interest would be foreigners who have no legal right to question the acts of the Crown in the Crown's courts as an act of state, as noted earlier. The author would not be able to obtain any legally binding order[102] to prevent an attack;[103] all he would be able to obtain, if anything, would be a legal declaration[104] that the Crown would be free to ignore. The only other option is to seek to persuade the Government to cease its readiness to attack, but Trident Ploughshares and others have tried strenuously in that regard and have had no success to date.

There are other factors supporting a relaxation of the requirement for an imminent danger: namely that (a) the crimes threatened, breach of the peace or malicious damage, are minor; (b) the harm caused by the accused would be minor in comparison to the harm threatened; (c) action now might be effective whereas action left until the danger is imminent could be futile; (d) in any case, waiting until the danger became imminent would be to create a situation where grave force was required and justified, including homicide.

The Requirements in this Case

If it is accepted that the requirement of imminent danger is simply part of the requirement that force is necessary and thus does not apply where

---

[101] There must be some legal right of the party at stake for a civil action to be taken in the courts: the party must have 'title' to sue. It is not enough that he is concerned for the fate of others: *Scottish Old People's Welfare Council [Age Concern Scotland], Petitioners* 1987 SLT 179.

[102] 'Interdict'.

[103] Crown Proceedings Act 1947 (c. 44), ss. 21, 43, *McDonald v. Secretary of State for Scotland* 1994 SLT 692, 1994 SCLR 318.

[104] 'Declarator'.

the force in question remains necessary due to the unavailability of protection from the authorities, then the criteria would be the following: the action must relate specifically to Trident; there must be some relationship between the acts of the accused and Trident so that they directly hinder, obstruct or stop, or try to hinder, obstruct and stop, the operation of Trident. There must be a sincere and actual intent to try to hinder, obstruct and stop the operation of Trident through those acts: protests or actions merely of a symbolic nature would be insufficient. Thus someone reaching a Trident submarine and painting slogans on it, or ringing the bell, are engaged in more symbolic acts whereas people setting out to damage the aerials, oxygen systems, or other key systems are doing as much as they can to stop the operation of Trident. Actions of a less direct nature, such as damaging a test barge or engaging in a blockade are more difficult and the cases would be likely to turn upon the beliefs of the accused as to what effect their actions would have, assessed with the likelihood of any real obstruction of Trident in mind.[105] Provided that a direct relationship and intent are present, if the defence the author has postulated exists (which is a huge 'if'), then the defence should be available to the accused.

Conclusion

The postulated defence faces various difficulties: primary amongst them being the question of justiciability of the deployment of armed forces, act of state doctrine, whether the defence of soldier's duty can be tenably extended to include most acts of armed conflict but not Trident, and whether self-defence is available to direct activists. What the author has hoped to do is introduce the reader to his arguments on these points, and to show that there is something worth looking into. Whether the

---

[105] That is to say, intent would be assessed objectively. If an activist professed a credible belief that his acts might have put Trident out of operation., this might still be disregarded if the court felt there was no real basis in fact for holding that belief. See for example *R v. Hill, R v. Hall* (1989) 89 Cr App Rep 74 where fence-cutting was held to be too remote as a matter of law as to constitute an effort to protect property from nuclear attack.

judges agree is another question, but what the author hoped to demonstrate is that there remains a rational basis for saying that use of nuclear weapons would not only be immoral but would be illegal as well, and that people can take action to prevent the illegal harm that could be brought about. Weapons of mass destruction are unique in that they are the only weapons that can be said in all instances by a single use to be virtually certain of killing substantial numbers of non-combatants. Municipal law allows the State to take risks with people's lives in certain circumstances and use physical, sometimes lethal, force against those who act against it: what it does not permit is a general right for the State to place its interests over those of others. Unlike the situation under international law, there is no right to kill for the State. The history of nuclear weapons is accompanied by a history of resistance with the resulting history of litigation. If activists are prepared to continue in the face of continuous prosecution, they might as well continue to seek new avenues to argue the justice of their actions and the injustice of their punishment, and they should give it the best shot they can. The author humbly suggests that the argument set out in this work is a new avenue worth navigating.[106]

---

[106] Those wishing to find out more about this defence are advised to look up the footnotes of this article. For a translation of these, see H. L. MacQueen, *Studying Scots Law,* 2nd Edt., (W. Green, 1998).

CHRONOLOGY: NUCLEAR WEAPONS IN SCOTLAND

August 1945   First atomic bomb used in warfare (Hiroshima, Japan)

1947   Attlee government decides to develop nuclear weapons.

1950   Aldermaston airfield becomes site for UK nuclear weapons programme.

October 1952   Britain's first nuclear explosion rises above Monte Bello Island.

January 1955   The first of Britain's V-bombers enters service.

October 1956   First British nuclear bomb (Blue Danube) dropped over South Australia.

1958   British Nuclear Fuels Ltd nuclear plant opened in Chapelcross, Dumfries-shire. Violet Club, an interim megaton weapon, enters service.

February 1960   British government decides that air- and submarine-launched missiles will be used. This decision amended on 13 April, when the UK abandoned development of submarine-launched missiles and opted for V-bombers armed with the new American Skybolt missile.

1961   Yellow Sun Mk2 enters service and was Britain's first service thermonuclear weapon. Blue Steel, Britain's first service nuclear missile, also enters service.

March 1961   The US Navy's Polaris fleet enters the Holy Loch to establish forward operating base. Scotland's relationship with the sea-borne deterrent begins.

April 1963   Polaris Sales Agreement signed between UK and US. Faslane Bay on the Gare Loch chosen as homeport for British Polaris SSBNs. Royal Dockyard at Rosyth in Fife chosen to refit nuclear-powered submarines. RNAD Coulport to be constructed on Loch Long.

1964	Polaris Chevaline project begins.
1966	WE 177 free-fall bomb enters service.
October 1967	Resolution class Polaris submarine, HMS *Resolution*, commissioned.
August 1967	Clyde Submarine Base, HMS *Neptune*, officially commissioned.
September 1968	Resolution class Polaris submarine, HMS *Repulse*, commissioned.
November 1968	Resolution class Polaris submarine, HMS *Renown*, commissioned.
June 1969	Responsibility for Britain's strategic nuclear deterrent passes to the Polaris submarines of the Royal Navy.
December 1969	Resolution class Polaris submarine, HMS *Revenge*, commissioned.
July 1980	Britain announces decision to purchase US Trident I C4 missile system. Significantly larger than its Polaris predecessor, plans to accommodate system at both Faslane and Coulport are made.
March 1982	Trident I C4 order cancelled by Britain. Decision to purchase US Trident II D5 missile system announced.
Mid-1982	First Chevaline equipped Polaris submarine sent on patrol.
September 1982	Trident nuclear missile service base to be built at Coulport near Helensburgh cancelled. Agreement with US government allows for Coulport's intended duties to be handled in King's Bay, Georgia.
April 1986	First Trident submarine (HMS *Vanguard*) ordered by the British government.
May 1986	£220 million reconstruction programme announced for the Royal Dockyard at Rosyth in Fife to handle refits of the Trident submarine fleet.
June 1987	Conservative government re-elected - Trident

	programme to proceed
December 1991	The Soviet Union officially came to an end. Trident programme continues in West of Scotland.
March 1992	Britain's first Vanguard class Trident SSBN, HMS *Vanguard* launched. Last US Navy ship leaves the Holy Loch after a presence of thirty-one years.
September 1992	Vanguard class Trident submarine refit competition between Rosyth Dockyard in Fife and Devonport Dockyard in Plymouth begins.
September 1993	Vanguard class Trident submarine, HMS *Victorious*, launched.
June 1993	£5 billion Trident refitting contract taken from Rosyth Dockyard and awarded to Devonport Dockyard
August 1993	Trident support facility, HM *Naval Base Clyde*, at Faslane opened by Secretary of State for Defence, Malcolm Rifkind.
December 1994	First operational patrol by Trident submarine (HMS *Vanguard*)
October 1995	Vanguard class Trident submarine, HMS *Vigilant*, launched.
December 1995	HMS *Victorious* enters service.
May 1996	Last Resolution class Polaris submarine decommissioned, Trident assumes responsibility of national deterrent.
January 1998	Cost of running Britain's nuclear deterrent roughly £1 billion a year according to Central Government
May 1999	Fourth Vanguard class Trident submarine, HMS *Vengeance*, expected to arrive at Faslane.

ABBREVIATIONS

ACE	Allied Command Europe
ADM	Atomic Demolition Munitions
BRIXMIS	British Military Mission
BNFL	British Nuclear Fuels Ltd
CND	Campaign for Nuclear Disarmament
CP	Communist Party
CPGB	Communist Party of Great Britain
CPX	Command Post Exercises
DAC	Direct Action Committee
D.S. 19	Defence Secretariat 19
FOR	Fellowship of Reconciliation
IAEA	International Atomic Energy Agency
ICC	International Criminal Court
ICJ	International Court of Justice
MAD	Mutually Assured Destruction
MFV	Motor Fishing Vehicle
NAAFI	Navy, Army and Air Force Institutes
NATO	North Atlantic Treaty Organisation
NBC	Nuclear, Biological and Chemical
NFLA	Nuclear Free Local Authorities
NORTHAG	Northern Army Group Headquarters
NUM	National Union of Mineworkers
POL	Petroleum, Oil and Lubricants
RNAD	Royal Navy Armaments Depot
SCAT	Scottish Campaign Against Trident
SCND	Scottish Campaign for Nuclear Disarmament
SCRAM	Scottish Campaign to Resist the Atomic Menace
SLBM	Submarine Launched Ballistic Missile
SNP	Scottish National Party
SOXMIS	Soviet Military Mission
SSBN	Nuclear Powered Ballistic Missile Submarine
STUC	Scottish Trades Union Congress
TCHD Mk2	Truck Cargo Heavy-Duty Mark 2
TEWT	Tactical Exercises Without Troops
TUC	Trade Union Congress

Cualann Press Titles

The Burns Boys
Alistair Renwick
ISBN 0 9544416 2 1: £12.99

Gurkha Reiver: Walking the Southern Upland Way
Neil Griffiths
ISBN 0 9544416 0 5: £10.99

Full Circle: Log of the Navy's No. 1 Conscript
John Gritten. Foreword Dr Peter Liddle, Director, The Second World War Experience, Leeds
ISBN 0 9535036 9 0: £19.99 Hardback

Coasting around Scotland
Nicholas Fairweather. Foreword Robin Harper MSP
ISBN 0 9535036 8 2: £12.99

Of Fish and Men: Tales of a Scottish Fisher
David C Watson Ph.D. Foreword Derek Mills
ISBN 0 9535036 3 1: £10.99

In Search of Willie Patterson: A Scottish Soldier in the Age of Imperialism
Fred Reid Ph.D. Foreword Professor Hamish Fraser
ISBN 09535036 7 4: £10.99

The Lion and the Eagle: Reminiscences of Polish Second World War Veterans in Scotland
Editor: Dr Diana M Henderson LLB TD FSA Scot. Foreword Dr Stanislaw Komorowski
ISBN: 0 9535036 4 X: £9.99

Stand By Your Beds! A Wry Look at National Service
David Findlay Clark OBE, MA, Ph.D., C..Psychol., F.B.Ps.S. Preface Trevor Royle, historian
ISBN: 0 9535036 6 6: £13.99

Open Road to Faraway: Escapes from Nazi POW Camps 1941-1945
Andrew Winton D A (Edin). Foreword Allan Carswell, Curator, National War Museum of Scotland
ISBN: 0 9535036 5 8: £9.99

Beyond the Bamboo Screen: Scottish Prisoners of War under the Japanese
Tom McGowran OBE. Foreword and Illustrations G S Gimson QC
ISBN 0 9535036 1 5: £9.99

On Flows the Tay: Perth and the First World War
Dr Bill Harding Ph.D., FEIS, Foreword Alan Hamilton, *The Times* journalist and author
ISBN 0 9535036 2 3: £12.99